A TEFLER'S Tale

The story of a language school

Michael Wills

www.fast-print.net/store.php

A TEFLER's Tale
Copyright © Michael Wills 2012

ISBN 978-178035-351-7

First published 2012 by
FASTPRINT PUBLISHING
Peterborough, England.

First published in the United Kingdom in 2012 by Michael Wills.

Michael Wills has asserted the moral right to be identified as the author of this work.

Contents

This book is dedicated to all those who helped to make my dream become a reality.

Preface

The danger of writing memoirs is that one can give the impression that a life's tale is complete. I sincerely hope that this is not the case. My purpose in writing this account of the evolution, trials and tribulations and the eventual success of the Salisbury School of English and connecting it with earlier events in my life which were instrumental in forming me into the person I am today, is to answer the call from many of my family and friends at various times, to document what actually happened. I chronicle the story of how lucky I have been in my choice of partner, who continued to believe in me even in the darkest of days, the wonderful support from my daughters all of whom are really children of the school, and lastly but by no means least the loyalty and respect of my colleagues and clients.

The EFL world is a particularly rich well to draw on when it comes to reminiscences which are seemingly too bizarre to be true, but I assure the reader that as far as I can remember, and with guidance from my work- and personal diaries, this is how it happened. However, a review of the contents of my work diaries from 1980 onwards made it abundantly clear that I would have to be selective in my account, otherwise the book would be of gargantuan length.

Henry Ford used to boast that when he arrived in Detroit he had nothing but the clothes on his back and his rucksack. When asked later what was in the rucksack he is said to have replied, "two hundred and fifty thousand dollars". Well, here I relate exactly what was in our rucksack when we started and where it came from. When we sold the business we did not make a vast fortune, but EFL was very, very good to us in so many other ways.

I have chosen to relate the happenings in the first three formative years year by year, and then later I summarise tales of people, significant places, things and events in topic areas rather than in chronological order. Finally, in the last years before my retirement I revert to a more detailed account.

I hope that this story may give others considering going into business some encouragement while sounding a warning bell to those who think that growing a company is easy.

MW

Salisbury April 2012

Cover page   TEFLER = Teacher of English as a foreign language

The cover photo shows the family moving into Rollestone Street after selling our home in Whiteparish.

Chapter 1   1979 and before

The stench of the mouse sitting on my arm awoke me. We looked at each other and then I flicked my gaze to Hercules, the family cat, who was sleeping contentedly on the floor in this, the only heated room in the house. I propelled the mouse to the mat in front of the recumbent feline form and simultaneously shouted "Hercules". He, the hunter, clearly felt that being presented with a quarry did not constitute sport and just watched as the reprieved mouse scurried across to the ill-fitting skirting board where it had been sheltering from the first frost of autumn.

I had been sleeping on a camp bed in the only furnished, but also the only un-refurbished room in what was, for another week, our ten room house. Apart from a cat which really only had loyalty to the house and not to me, I had the very basic necessities for a Spartan bachelor life. These included one cup, one plate and a knife and fork and such foodstuffs as reflected my culinary ineptitude.

In a week's time after legal completion I would be following my wife, Barbro, and three daughters to Winchester to start a new life and a new business. They had left a month earlier so that the two older girls, Anna and Sarah could start school at the beginning of term. Emma was not yet two.

Ann Walsh at our 25th anniversary party

We had spent five years and far too much money on what at times seemed a totally all consuming, overambitious project to restore a nineteenth century wooden manor house to its former glory. The profit from this enterprise, which amounted to £18,000, together with a loan of £12,000 from a dear friend, Ann Walsh, whose level of trust in us was hugely appreciated but really quite worrying, was to provide the capital thought to be needed, (and grossly underestimated), for our business venture and most of our living expenses until the School could provide an income for us.

We had a little in the way of residual income from various enterprises I had embarked on in Sweden and some royalties from the books I had written with EFL colleagues. In the last five years of my time in Sweden I had been involved as manager in a publishing venture set up to serve the creative efforts of teachers working for the Educational Trust which I had been employed by since moving to Sweden in 1965. The Chairman of the Board of the local branch of the Trust was extremely supportive and understanding. I was new to this business environment and I had a lot to learn, but he was patient and also realised that I needed the extra stimulation of contact with teaching and teachers. Because of this he allowed me the option of occasional unpaid leave to engage in teaching and writing projects as opportunities arose.

While the publishing house had initially been a profitable enterprise for the Trust with a number of innovative language training publications, increasing pressure was put on the Board, and thus on me, by the non- language teaching arm of the organisation to publish more and more fanciful titles and specialist interest books such as "Are We Alone In Space?", which I knew could never be made profitable with our limited marketing resources, and indeed were not. This led to a measure of disenchantment on my part, but the job did give me very useful business experience and a lot of ideas, contacts and opportunities for my extra-curricular activities.

I had set up a company which I ran in my spare time, called International Language Services, (ILS), the main purpose of which was to import EFL books direct from England. I supplied branches of the Educational Trust in various parts of the country. Their problem was that they did not know until student enrolments came in at the beginning of each term what numbers of various titles they would need. Once their requirement was known they needed the books fast. In order to overcome the long delays and high mark-ups of conventional bookshops I imported direct from a UK wholesaler, later to become a great friend, in Bournemouth. This worked very well initially, but I realised that sooner or later these customers would want to bypass me and go direct to the supplier and I could not prevent it. This indeed happened eventually and while I did still have some customers in October 1979, the business was very much in decline.

During my final year in Sweden I had helped to initiate a project with a training company called Basicon to produce a comprehensive set of materials designed for courses to equip Swedish businesses with an in-depth knowledge of British life, commerce and institutions with a view to increasing exports to the UK. The project, called Marketing to Britain, (MTB), was financed by the Swedish Department of Trade and Industry. I commissioned a number of writers to help, including Hazel Lake, who was later to become instrumental in developing our school in England. Hazel had been a star teacher at the Trust in Uppsala, but had returned to the UK for personal reasons.

By this time we had made public our intention to set up a school in Winchester and the intention was that the participants studying on the MTB project would attend part of their courses at the school. This should get us off to a flying start.

Another venture which produced a welcome income source for a while during the transitional stage between the security of a regular income in Sweden and the hoped for return on our investment in England, was a joint one between my Swedish employer and the wholesale book supplier in Bournemouth, called Language Teaching Resources, (LTR). The Trust had published an innovative English teaching material system written by a team of my colleagues and me which attempted to address the difficulty in adapting teaching books to the real needs and interests of individual classes. It was called Your Choice.

In short, instead of using a text book with a fixed content, a teacher could order a selection of lesson materials in folded A3 format, chosen from a menu. These lessons were sold in a purpose designed ring binder for each student. LTR had been set up to adapt and publish this material for the international market. The project was, unfortunately, to be short-lived. Within a year of my returning to the UK the company was wound up. While the principle of choice was very popular with teachers, it was a commercial failure because of the high cost of collation and distribution.

In forming our business plan for our proposed school in Winchester I was lulled into a false sense of certainty that my broad range of contacts in the adult educational field in Scandinavia, (I had some contacts in Norway, and in particular in Denmark where the Trust had produced a bespoke language course for the National Banking Association), would provide a steady stream of business for us. With the naivety of those of high principles and little experience we had decided to initially shun the possibility of running group adult courses and more especially to avoid for ever the teenage market, which we regarded as over exploited and the road to perdition. Our intention was to run teachers' courses, private one-to-one courses and specialist business courses such as MTB.

By the end of May 1979 we had negotiated with the landlord the basis of a lease for the first and second floor of premises in central Winchester, opposite the Butter Cross. We had also registered a company called the Winchester School of English Limited. For our own accommodation we had, in April, with a minimal deposit, bought a house at Oliver's Battery, a new development to the west of the City. The house was small indeed, but we intended to shoe-horn ourselves into this modest accommodation.

On arrival in Winchester I was greeted with the news that the District Council had refused permission for a change of use of our proposed premises from office to educational use. The landlord was livid and offered to appeal at his own expense. However, this would take at least five months and even if successful we would be too late to start promoting the School for the following summer. This would delay the time when we might expect some income to stop the depletion of our capital.

Things looked bleak and instead of launching ourselves into preparing premises for a school to open in November, we found ourselves unemployed, apart from the diminishing book business. If Winchester was not ready for a language school then we would look elsewhere. Within a week we had found likely premises in Salisbury and a reasonable welcome from the Planning Department to our enquiry about a change to educational use. Indeed, it soon became clear that the City planners were keen for 14 Rollestone Street to be occupied as it was situated in a prime location and had been empty for two years. This also explained why the landlords, a gang of local business grandees, who were later described to us as "greedy men" by one of their own, were so keen to ensnare a tenant and why, on our part, meagre means and lack of references were no barrier to fulfilling this aim. Their bait was a reduction of two thousand pounds in the rent for the first year to three thousand, and the sentence was a 21 year full repairing lease with three yearly upward only rent reviews.

On the plus side it was a fine old Queen Ann building in the centre of the city - but prime amongst the negatives, the previous tenants, a firm of solicitors obviously did not have the same requirements as us in relation to the standard of appearance of the rooms. There was much to be done to bring the décor up to an acceptable standard. A further matter of concern was that the town bus station was just opposite the premises and that there might be issues about noise and fumes.

We instructed our solicitor, (an overstatement really as we had no solicitor, but we had used the one who did the conveyancing for our doll's house in Winchester, I. B.). He offered us a "special" deal to act in the matter of a lease on the Salisbury premises. Just how special this deal was, would become apparent later.

The weeks of delay dragged into months while we waited for the lease to be completed. I had no experience of such matters, but in retrospect I believe that our file was allowed to collect dust in both the landlord's and prospective tenant's solicitors' offices. During this period we registered the name Salisbury School of English and released the name Winchester School of English. (The latter name was later picked up by colleagues in Winchester and a school was eventually started there in 1989, though not in our intended premises).

The interior of Rollestone Street after refurbishment.
Left – entrance hall with my office furthest in
Right – the upstairs hall

A particular difficulty for us was that because of the uncertainty about where our school would be, we could not produce promotional material and begin marketing. And, related to this, the hiatus caused a number of possible business leads with my Swedish contacts to go cold.

At last, in the first week of December a call came from our solicitor to say that the lease was ready for signing and that we could take over the premises on 1st January 1980. By this time we were reconciled to commuting the 30 miles from Winchester to Salisbury each day and the need for a huge effort to refurbish the premises in order to open at Easter 1980.

I had the tremendous good fortune to call in a favour from the co-owner of a national newspaper to whom I had previously given advice about an educational publication for children. He agreed to put an advertising leaflet about teachers' courses in a mailing to all European schools. This got us our first enrolments for a course to be held in the summer and one single enrolment for a course at Easter.

A school needs teachers, but with our capital we could not afford to employ anyone on a fixed contract before we had a steady flow of students and that was a long way off. We had no group business in the pipeline from Sweden, mainly because of the time lag in setting up the School, but we did have some tentative company enquiries about private tuition. I intended to teach the one-to-one students from these companies, but I needed two better qualified teachers to run the teachers' courses. Ann, my business partner, had extensive experience of teachers' courses from her time at International House in London. She had offered to work part time in the summer, but could not commit herself long term because of her family and business interests.

My own academic background was weak in relation to English as a foreign language. While I had qualified teacher status in the UK and had attended a month long EFL course in Sweden, my main strengths were fourteen years of EFL teaching and several years in educational administration. In fact it was other skills which were initially, and indeed continuously, of great importance too.

Having failed my eleven plus exam at the primary school I had attended on the Isle of Wight, a school called Barton Juniors and whose past pupils were, (and still are), labelled "Barton bone heads" by the local community, who in turn were known as caulk heads by overners on the mainland, I was cast as an academic no hoper and sent to a brand new secondary modern school, Priory Boys School, at Carisbrooke. My chum Bill Kittle and I thrived on this lack of expectation of academic achievement and embarrassed the system by gaining so many GCE passes that we were both transferred to a grammar school which had just been built next door. At the age of sixteen the environment of a Grammar School suited me well, not least being the first co-educational establishment I had studied in. However, having missed the first five years of this type of education Bill and I felt like interlopers and were made to feel so by many of the teachers who resented yoicks from the neighbouring school being thrust upon them. No quarter was given. For example, I was placed in a Latin class where all the other pupils had studied Latin for five years while I had been doing gardening, woodwork and metalwork, and the situation was similar for other subjects.

When the time came to consider my future, I explained to the Careers Master that I had a great interest in the sciences and I would like to make a career in the new branch called "electronics". "Nonsense", he told me, "there is no future in electronics, in a few years machines will take over. What about becoming a teacher?"

And so it was that I entered the teaching profession. My parents would never have had an expectation that I would become other than a manual worker of some sort and even if they had thought otherwise they would not have known how to coach me to pass the eleven plus. (As we, quite unashamedly, did our daughters!). However, as I was to discover, nothing aids social mobility better than higher education, and this was the path, albeit at a modest level, that this Barton bonehead was to take.

But to go back to the Priory Boys School experience; I had learned and become quite proficient in practical skills such as carpentry, decorating and electrical engineering. These abilities have served me very well all my life and in particular in rescuing old buildings from a lack of tender loving care.

As I said earlier, my academic background would not impress a school authority looking to entrust teachers to a course in Salisbury. I had been fortunate enough to work with many gifted and well qualified teachers in Sweden and one of them, already mentioned, Hazel Lake, agreed to join our fledgling enterprise. Not only would she teach, but also help with the refurbishment of the building, all for the princely wage of £3.40 per hour. However, Hazel needed accommodation as her home was in Harlow and so our first priority was to make a dilapidated flat on the second floor habitable without spending too much of our precious capital. Fortunately, Hazel had simple tastes and accepted living in one room and using a bathroom which seemed to have successfully avoided advances in the science of plumbing for a great many years.

Our next task was for Barbro and Hazel to set about painting and wall-papering while I lined all the undulating floors with hardboard so that they could be carpeted. But let me first describe the building.

As I have previously related, the building showed little sign of having been loved in the recent past. The ground floor was reasonably presentable as presumably clients had been entertained there by the previous incumbents. The impressive front door opened into a minute, and obviously recently built, porch. This, we quickly realised, having taken tenancy in the winter, had been constructed to minimise the effects of cold blasts of air often carrying the noxious fumes of the buses opposite. This sacrificed the possibility of a visitor getting a notable first impression of the fine entrance hall and the imposing staircase. To the left of the hall was the largest room in the building which was to become the student lounge. To the right a tiny kitchen and storeroom. The visitor neglecting the room to the left and the kitchen to the right would proceed down a short corridor and find further rooms left and right. The former, which was wooden panelled, was to become the main office and the latter a one-to-one classroom. This room had a window that looked out on a much-overshadowed garden patch some three metres by three.

Straight ahead down the corridor was a one-storey twentieth century add-on room also affording a view of the "garden". This room had a door on the other side that gave access to a small courtyard with high walls. This facility was less than an amenity at the beginning of our tenure, being covered to a depth of many inches with the by-product of what must have been the total pigeon population of Wiltshire if not Wessex.

The first floor had a large central hall with high ceilings and a planked floor which was so uneven that it was redolent of a lake with ripples on. There were four good sized classrooms accessed from the four corners of the hall. One of them had a huge walk in safe with a locking handle on the outside. Anyone venturing into this safe could easily be locked in by anyone with malevolent intent on the outside, as indeed happened on more than one occasion. There was also a small room with a floor which sloped gently from one side to the other. Initially we used this as my office but I found that the gradient caused my office chair which was on casters, to gradually glide further and further from my desk. On reversing the arrangement and moving my office work place to the opposite wall the chair pinned me to the desk instead.

The whole first floor felt strangely too spacious to anyone who had explored the ground floor. It was in fact twice the width of the ground floor as it covered the ground floor of an adjoining property. We had a "flying leasehold"! (My knowledge of estate agents vernacular had increased spectacularly in the hunt for premises, though my favourite term was that for the panelling which reached half way up the walls of most rooms to "dado height". Though I never did discover what a dado might be).

The top floor was mainly derelict with much crumbling plasterwork and ceilings. It had clearly once been a fine five room flat though probably not within living memory. From this floor there was a short series of steps which led on to a flat part of the roof.

Under the building was an extensive cellar in part of which another large metal walk-in safe had been constructed. Access to the cellar was down a stairway from the ground floor or through a sunken doorway at the front of the building. The cellar ceiling was not lined and the underside of the ground floor floorboards, complete with gaps, were visible from below. Thus a generous supply of cold air flowed from the cellar to the rooms above whenever the sunken door was opened.

The whole pile was heated by an eccentric system of off-peak heaters. These contraptions, which looked like, and were as big as, medium sized refrigerators on their sides, worked on the principle that they used electricity at night when it was cheapest. Dense bricks inside the appliances were thus heated and in theory would exude cheery warmth through the day. This they did irrespective of the ambient temperature. On a reasonable autumn day, once the early morning chill had worn off, they functioned and felt like a sauna heater. On a winter's day they would generously dissipate their therms by mid-morning and hungrily await a new cheap electric charge the following night.

In both cases this made choosing a wardrobe to work in the office or indeed to study in a classroom quite difficult as in the autumn and spring the inexperienced occupant would arrive at school heavily clad in expectation of a typical cold English interior only to find a hothouse environment which cooled to comfortable by afternoon. In the winter, light clothing was in order in the mornings and thermals in the afternoon.

To have brought this building up to the standard we aspired to in the short term would have sent us to the bankruptcy court in no time at all, so we determined to accept shortcomings such as the heating system as quaint features for later attention and to concentrate on improving the general décor with such time, money and skills as we had.

There was one exception however, and that was the need for an understanding and possible overhaul of the arcane electrical wiring system. This was way beyond the scope of what I had learnt at school. The cabling from different nooks and crannies in each room snaked back towards a small walk-in cupboard on the ground floor. Various wires, clearly of different epochs, some covered in lead, some in wound cotton and some in ancient plastic, weaved their tortuous way round doors, under floors and other places which never saw the light of day until they eventually, in one curling tangle, disappeared into a distribution box of large proportions which had been sealed like a pharaoh's sarcophagus by the generous application of paint by many generations of decorators.

I found an electrician in Yellow Pages called Mr Coombes. He seemed completely at one with this electrical mystery and gallimauphry of wires. I never asked his age, but it was considerable. I mused that perhaps this cornucopia of cables awoke nostalgia in him for his long ago apprenticeship which had prepared him to understand the nature of such geriatric wiring. After much prodding with an instrument he called his "megger", which had the appearance of historical items which I have seen in the Science Museum, he declared the system fit for purpose.

Barbro was queen of the office, presiding over our manual Swedish typewriter and second-hand Xerox copier. She dealt with all student enquiries, (initially a less than daunting chore), promotion, the building up of a host family register and child care, (with an increasingly active Emma), often with a paint brush in hand. At 14.15 each day she would rush off to drive to Winchester to collect the other two girls from school.

By Easter 1980 we had generally smartened up the ground floor, the toilets and a couple of classrooms on the first floor. The floors were resplendent with new brown carpet. Furniture had been obtained from second hand stores, bankruptcy sales and from our much overstocked little house. On the 25th March, a week before Easter our brochures arrived from the printers. We were ready for business!

Chapter 2   1980   A School is born

As I bent over the spade I had the uneasy feeling that something was wrong. Glancing behind me I was horrified to see a tumble of blonde hair framing a suntanned, not unpleasing, face poking out towards me through the open lower sash window. Our first student had arrived early and had found her way to what it transpired was the only source of noise around the building! Me digging!

It was Tuesday morning 1st April 1980. We had advertised a one week teachers' refresher course to take place over Easter from Wednesday. Though we had only received one enrolment we had decided to run the course anyway. It was our first and only income so far and as Mao said, "great journeys always begin with a small first step".

We knew that our student Monica, a German teacher, would arrive at her host family on Tuesday, the day before the course, so we were busy putting the finishing touches to such parts of the building which were presentable and would be used in the next week. I felt that these finishing touches were now reaching absurd proportions when I succumbed to the repeated cajoling of the two women staff to do something with our "garden". It will be recalled that the garden measured some three by three metres and could only be accessed through the windows of two of the ground floor rooms.

I had bought a honeysuckle plant and a few pansies. I put on my overalls and ventured through the window, complete with gardening implements and the plants. I was surprised that there was a drop of around one and a half metres onto the much untended soil and made a mental note that it would be quite difficult to get back in again. I was thus employed when it seems that Monica had wandered in through the front door and evaded the staff. As I later learned, both Barbro and Hazel had decided to go to the market to buy some flowers to put in the classrooms. Their enthusiasm for this errand had overcome them to the extent that they had left the front door open and forgotten to tell me that they had gone out.

What do I do? It was obvious to me who the fair Teuton peering at me was, but I could not possibly tell her who I was and retain my dignity.

"I find no one in the school" she said.

"Argh, well I'm the gardener but there must be someone in the office miss". I fell easily into a Wiltshire accent, it not being far removed from the Isle of Wight accent which I had been suppressing all my adult life.

I made towards the window and called Barbro's name trying not to betray the panic I felt. After several calls with successively rising pitch and volume I decided that I would have to get back in through the window and find staff whose appearance might imbue more confidence in the organisation than that of my own. But how to get back in?

I abandoned my gardening paraphernalia and attempted a dignified scaling of the wall under the window. Monica immediately grabbed my muddy hand and with surprising strength helped to haul me through the window. The relief at hearing the voices of the two women in the hall very temporarily overcame my uncharitable thoughts about what I would say to them for putting me in this situation. I quickly introduced Monica before drawing Barbro aside and telling her in Swedish of the subterfuge that I was the gardener. Her amusement did little to assuage my temper. I asked her to tell Hazel before I was undone.

I returned to my horticultural endeavours taking with me a small step ladder to ensure my eventual escape. Meanwhile the ever resourceful Hazel, on hearing of my plight from Barbro, explained to Monica that today was April fool's day and I had a wicked sense of humour which included passing myself off as the gardener.

Clearly this was "embarrass the Principal day". After I had successfully completed my task and cleaned up we invited Monica to come with us to our local pub just across the road, the Pheasant, for lunch.

The bar was crowded, for in those pre-yogurt at the desk halcyon days, office workers took an hour's lunch and quite frequently met in the pub. Having fought my way through the throng to gain a vantage point at the counter, I called back to the ladies to ask what they would like to drink. Monica shouted "A pint of milk". The crowd fell almost silent while people turned to see who had made the joke. I realised that Monica was probably serious.

Now, in these health conscious days when it is quite de rigueur to order soft drinks or a cup of tea in a pub this would not be noteworthy. But in the early eighties a pub was not the place to go to for a drink of milk. So my discomfort was amplified when my turn came to be served, the moment the other customers had been waiting for. Above the babble of voices and the wail of the juke box I shouted "A pint of bitter, two halves of shandy and", my voice dropping to pianissimo "a pint of milk".

"And what mate?"

"A pint of milk"

"Sorry mate can't let you have a pint, I'll see how much they can spare from the kitchen."

Eventually, Monica got the best part of half a pint and we ordered food. I could go on to describe in detail how Monica's ham and cheese omelette had to be returned to the kitchen amid much fuss and assertiveness which included the classic "I asked to become a ham and cheese omelette", as she felt that there was insufficient ham for it to justify the title.

We had our first student and we had begun to ascend the learning curve. Needless to say we gave the Pheasant a miss for a few days as I felt that providing lunch time entertainment to the locals was not part of my remit.

The period between Easter and the summer was very quiet apart from the necessary administration work of building up the accommodation register, setting up admin routines and servicing enquiries. And there were some!

The proprietors ready for business

The enquiries we received related to proposed teachers courses which were publicised as an enclosure in the school magazines published by the national newspaper.

It had become clear to me, that if I were to manage the school efficiently and have time to work with promotion, I could not teach full time. On 23rd May I interviewed a prospective local teacher, Gill Pitt, and offered her some part time summer teaching, at the same rate as Hazel.

However, at our pre-summer meeting on 12th June, Ann announced to Hazel and me that because of personal circumstances she would be unable to do much work in the summer. This was a blow as the three of us got on very well personally and professionally. She had anticipated our concern and told us that an old International House colleague of hers whom she held in high regard, Nick McIver, was moving to Salisbury because of an 'affair de coeur' and would be looking for work.

I met Nick on the 26th June for a chat. The meeting was at first uneasy, partly because of his healthy suspicion of all employers, and partly because it took a while for his natural charm to overcome the initial negative impression I formed from his bohemian appearance. This was to be the start of a friendship which endured and a professional relationship that lasted for my entire time at the School. It would be less than honest to say that the relationship was always smooth, more than once in the early years he told me that he would never work with me again, I think it fair to say that I recognised his outstanding talent before he recognised my abilities. Sadly, this great character is no longer with us, having died in 2011, a huge loss.

The relative pre-summer calm gave us the chance to continue with the work of refurbishing the building. We put in very long hours and spent far too much of our precious capital. It had become clear to us that the commute to and from Winchester each day was taking too much of our painting and decorating time. It also necessitated Barbro leaving work at half past two many afternoons to collect the children from their Winchester school.

Some afternoons our neighbours' Spanish au pair, Charro, collected the children, but we realised that it was unreasonable to depend on this and in any case there was a limit to the activities we could find to keep Emma entertained at our school while we were busy. She had developed a useful technique of hiding under the admin desk when visitors came in and really was very patient. It was almost as if she realised the importance of what we were about. But a long drive twice a day was stressful both for her and for Barbro, whose sense of direction had more than once led her to Southampton rather than Winchester.

There was also the expense of running two cars each day on the sixty mile round trip. We decided to put the house on the market and to move closer to Salisbury. The process went very smoothly and by August we had moved to the village of Whiteparish, just 5 miles from Salisbury. Our neighbours in Winchester had decided to emigrate and we inherited a now homeless Charro who moved with us. Though very useful to us, she had the most remarkable sense of time, or rather lack of sense of time. We could never really rely on her to be at the children's school on time to pick them up. It was a relief on those days when we did not to get a call from the school to say our children were waiting to be picked up. We got support from family too. In order to help us concentrate all our efforts on the summer school my parents-in-law had offered to have the three girls with them in Sweden through late July and August.

We were learning fast but not fast enough! One day in May an Iranian woman walked into the school and asked to enrol. She handed over a thousand pounds in notes and filled in an application form. She already had a visa so only required proof on enrolment. We could not believe it, there on the desk, a thousand pounds! Our joy was short lived when she returned a day later and said that she had changed her mind, she wanted her money back. We gave her every penny, as we had no proper terms and conditions which could justify us making a deduction. It was a disappointment but a good lesson.

Our summer comprised a succession of four, two week teachers' courses with an average of four or five students on each. A modest number, but it was real income at last. Nick, Hazel and Ann split the teaching between them. I taught the small number of one-to-one students and Gill taught a little group of "off the street" enrollers.

An oddity about my EFL career was that apart from a summer course for French teenagers in Brixham in 1966, I had only ever taught Scandinavian students. The Brixham experience is what probably had the greatest influence on my thinking that we should not run teenagers' courses in Salisbury. The teaching there had been pleasant enough, but the lack of out of school activities had led to a load of worries. Things came to a head when the leader, a Basque teacher with a physique like a front row rugby forward, lined the children up at the morning assembly and announced that several shop keepers had contacted him to say that goods had gone missing from their shops and they suspected that French children might be responsible. He gazed at the line of angelic faces and said, "If any of you have stolen anything from a shop will you please bring it to tomorrow's assembly so that I can return it."

This man was clearly not to be trifled with, for the next morning, half the group turned up carrying carrier bags containing items from shops, cafes and places of interest we had visited, including spoons from a monastery! The staff duly collected in the goods and the children were given absolution on threat of some extreme pestilence befalling them if they stole again.

The problem for us teachers then was what to do with the goods. We had no idea where most of the things had come from and we could hardly go around the town asking shopkeepers to identify their missing stock from the swag which had obviously been garnered from a wide geographical area. There was a definite risk that the interest of the Devon constabulary might be awakened.

That evening, over a few glasses of calvados, a solution was agreed on. We would hire a rowing boat, put all the goods in a weighted sack and dump it in Brixham harbour under cover of darkness.

And so, apart from this educational interlude in 1966, I was very much a Scandinavian teacher. This meant that although I could predict and cure the linguistic inadequacies of folk from the north, it was real learning experience for me to be faced with my first Italian student, a one-to-one post graduate called Teresa. However, the experience was very valuable and soon I had the chance to teach other nationalities too. It was tremendously rewarding and enjoyable, but as the summer wore on, the yawning chasm of the autumn and winter came closer. It was clear even to a novice businessman like me, that this was really not going to work unless we quickly diversified into other areas of EFL or found other income sources.

It is surprising how rapidly the experience of staring financial ruin in the face can overcome idealistic aims and stimulate business acumen. Despite our lofty ideals of only running teachers' courses and one-to-one classes, by September we were enrolling au pairs for group classes. However, the au pairs paid little and there was a real difficulty in finding times when they could all attend class at the same time. We were grasping at straws in every direction. We agreed to have the premises used as a "crammer" for English school children in the late afternoons and evenings. The latter included French courses for primary aged children. These were very successful until Alice, our extremely talented French teacher, moved from Salisbury. We also arranged accommodation for a French organisation which brought groups of school children for short stay trips to England. These students did not attend school, nor would we have allowed it. (In fact at this point in time we still vowed we would not get involved in teenagers courses, even though several teachers on our summer courses had asked if they could bring groups of their own pupils to the school next summer. We had politely, and in retrospect stupidly, told them that we would only accept adults). We even put up a sign outside the School offering photocopying services.

17

The "crammer" school gave us some rent, but I soon began to doubt its worth to us. I had to stay at the School until 20.00 four evenings each week to let people in and out and while this was no great hardship, it did mean that I could not do any useful work on the building as parents reasonably had an expectation that the person receiving their children would not be dressed as an artisan and possibly besmirched with paint.

To my intense relief some of my Swedish contacts started to come good, in particular I was indebted to my mother-in-law, who was Head of Administration of Uppsala College of Education, for a lead which gave us a series of courses for nurses. The first of which, happened in November. Generally though, autumn activity was far too sparse; we were losing money and lots of it.

To friends and family it must have seemed a crazy decision for us to have left the safe cocoon provided by the Swedish welfare state for this parlous existence. Barbro and I had agreed on the reasons and never once, even at the worst times did we seriously question our decision.

Sweden had given me a lot. Not only did I have the stunning opportunity to develop professionally from a novice TEFL teacher to a Director of Teacher Training and Development for a staff of over a hundred and twenty teachers and later a managing directorship in an educational publishers, but the opportunities for "extra" earnings in the cash rich educational environment of Sweden in the sixties and seventies, allowed me into the world of radio and even a television educational programme production. (The latter was short lived though, because I loudly criticised the musical score during a break in an acting recording not knowing that the primadonna composer was behind the lights and heard what I said). There were chances to do translations, write articles and most remunerative of all, to write schoolbooks.

The level of my earnings had allowed us to buy the manor house by a beautiful lake, with enough land to breed sheep and geese and to keep chicken. For the children it was, in many ways a halcyon existence in the country. We had fish in the lake, mutton for the pot and fresh free range eggs every day.

But with the children approaching English school age we were getting increasingly concerned that in Sweden they could not start school until the age of seven. Anna was already reading well and we really could not see why she should have to wait two more years before her formal education would start. When she reached her fifth birthday in April 1977 we decided to arrange for her to attend a private school in England and to stay with my parents near to the school in New Milton. This arrangement could not last however as we missed her dreadfully, (though I am not sure that this feeling was mutual as she took to school life wonderfully and was thoroughly spoiled by her grandparents), and also we felt that it was too great an imposition on my parents. So, when she returned to Sweden at Christmas 1977 we decided to apply for early entrance to a Swedish state pre-school. This had unexpected repercussions. Within a week we received a visit from two educational psychologists, ostensibly to examine Anna, but in fact I quickly recognised that they were more interested in what kind of parent could drive a five year-old so hard that not only could she read and write before she was supposed to, according to the great Swedish scheme of things, but also request that the child should be driven even harder by going to school a year and a half earlier than she should. The answer to our request was a firm no.

But there were other things, some of them in a sense related to the foregoing. At work I was finding the power and intrusiveness of the unions and the introduction almost weekly of new employment legislation, more and more limiting to running a small business. At times it was quite unbelievable the lengths I had to go to to make even small changes in staff job descriptions. Within the company, staff meeting after staff meeting lowered productivity and began to dampen my natural enthusiasm. The crunch came when I was threatened with union intervention when, quite innocently, I changed the type of coffee in the staff canteen.

The thing which worried me most was that the laudable principle of equality in everything was beginning to mean that excellence was frowned on. I saw it in the company, where for example, we were not allowed to suggest that one employee might be performing better than another. Everyone was equally good, it was just that some might require more training. This was reflected in an inability to reward individual achievement.

Equality was seen as a constituent part of democracy, which in turn had the most absurd manifestations. I recall going to the children's play school to see the celebration of the feast of St Lucia on 13th December. By tradition, one girl is chosen as Lucia and she has a candle bearing entourage of attendants with various roles, all dressed in white. Lucia wears a crown of (electric) candles. We parents all sat in the school hall and awaited the arrival of the procession. When it appeared, we were all taken aback to see twenty Lucias. The teacher made a serious announcement that in the interests of democracy all the children were given the part of Lucia.

I longed to be allowed to be more entrepreneurial. This is why I set up my own little company, International Language Services, with zero employees. It gave me the chance to try out my own ideas without the yoke of interminable conferences and consultations. And thus it was that we got the idea of starting our own business in the UK where, at that time, the life of an employer was much simpler than in Sweden. This, coupled with our concern about the children's education, set our plans in train.

And so it was that we now found ourselves in a penurious state in a vast Queen Ann mansion. There was no going back, or any thought of it. We had to succeed. But as we were to learn, nothing which is worth having comes without a price. And the first real test of our resilience was soon to come. We learnt through the years that one should beware of the euphoria created by pleasant experiences because disaster can always be lurking beyond it. October was to be a case in point.

In the autumn things were quiet, we had a few students as already mentioned and we were laying plans for the following summer. On 16th October one of those rare events occurred which was to have life shaping consequences. The manager of a local wine importers came in together with a young Italian man called Andrea Cecchi. She explained that he was the son of an Italian wine producer. He was staying with her and he needed to learn English. His parents would prefer him to have private tuition.

 For us this was the beginning of a fine long-term personal relationship with the Cecchi family, an awakening of curiosity about Italy which led to a deep affection for the country and last, but not least, a not inconsiderable amount of revenue as other members of Andrea's family and friends attended courses with us over the years.

We were still looking for new "quick fix" revenue streams. Through my work with the Marketing To Britain project I had got to know a manager at the Swedish Trade Council in London and in conversation he had once dropped in a comment about some English employees of Swedish companies in the UK needing basic Swedish. We hit on a plan to run a beginners' Swedish course for this target group. I was able to get a list of all Swedish companies with UK subsidiaries through my contacts with the Trade Council. We wrote a course description and did a mailing.

The response to the mailing was really encouraging, but showed the need for a course at elementary level too. I had good access to Swedish for Immigrants teaching materials from my time at the publishing house and Barbro set about adapting this material to suit our ends. We set prices at a level far higher than we were able to charge our EFL clients and planned a beginner's course for February 1981 and one elementary course in the same month with a further elementary course in May.

One afternoon Hazel pointed out to Barbro that the internal wooden panelling was cracking on the wall on the outside of which was the pigeon infested courtyard. This was probably the original panelling which dated from when the house was built and was a particularly fine feature. We all had a look at the panelling and I gave one of the cracks a little prod. The wood gave way and released a distinct and unpleasant smell. The hole revealed a cluster similar in appearance to a dense white spider's web. It was obvious that we had some form of fungal growth under the panelling.

Stupidly, I phoned the landlord's agent and asked if they had had any similar fungus before. It was not many minutes before the man arrived hotfoot with a very affluent looking companion who was introduced to us as the landlord's building surveyor. He gave the air of one who has done very well out of surveying. "Dry rot", he said, "it is endemic in Salisbury, the city is riddled with spores, but it only develops if the conditions are right".

Contrary to my first impression that this dapper gentleman would seldom get his hands dirty he launched himself with gusto at the yet undisturbed panelling. We watched in horror as the surveyor pulled off several panels, each one revealing the same foul tendrils. I must have blanched visibly at the thought of the cost of eradicating this and rebuilding the panelling.

"Bad luck Mr Wills", the agent intoned like an undertaker, "under the terms of your full repairing lease this is your responsibility".

The surveyor cheerfully added by way of comfort, "Don't worry, you can get advice on what to do to eradicate this from the District Council. You are legally required to report to them any outbreak of dry rot." This filled me with dread as I had a vision of the Council requiring that we remove all the panelling in the building to check the extent of the infestation. On a more helpful note he gave me the phone number of a building firm which had experience of this type of thing.

The pair bade farewell and as they left, the surveyor, with the air of one who can now return to his office and raise an invoice, added, "Call me when you have had the panelling reinstated and I will inspect it for the landlord".

I duly made the phone call to the Council and was relieved to be told that they did not have the resources to inspect the site but that I should call them when the outbreak had been dealt with, and oh yes, in order to avoid spreading the spores the infected wood must be burnt on the site of the outbreak. How we could do this I did not know. A bonfire in our three by three garden next to a Grade two listed building would not be a good idea.

The building firm sent a man in overalls which were much cleaner than mine. Perhaps he had them washed each week or maybe he never got them dirty. I felt that I would have been at some advantage had I had mine on to show that I was a kindred spirit and thus might mitigate the size of the quote. After much sucking of teeth and sniffing of the part of the office which had not been subjected to the vandalism of the surveyor, he declared that he thought that the dry rot had only affected the part of the room with an outside wall. He verified what the man in the suit had said about the fact that the conditions have to be right for this pestilence to thrive. The conditions required were warmth and damp. We could see where the warmth was coming from, for the first time for several years there was heating in the room. But where was the damp coming from?

The overalled artisan asked to see the outside wall. This meant a foray into the pigeon besmirched courtyard which could only be accessed from my office. He ventured into the foul smelling area treading carefully but ineffectively as the mess was unavoidable. Climbing back up through the door and leaving a trail of muck on my new carpet he announced that the problem was that the building had been constructed before the introduction of damp courses and that water could travel up through the wall from the wet courtyard. The solution was, according to him, that we put in an artificial damp course. This could be done by drilling a large number of holes on the brickwork and irrigating the holes with a fluid which would set and form an impregnable barrier. But before they could do any work, the yard would have to be cleaned as it was currently a health hazard.

I was so relieved at his relatively simple solution to the damp proofing that I was more than willing to accede to his request about the cleaning. I had intended to do it anyway of course, but it was way down the priority list.

Further, he would put in his quote a sum for the removal of the remaining panelling from the infected wall, scraping away the plant life and re-panelling the room. I saw a chance to save some expense and asked him to quote only for the damp course. I would remove the panelling and the fungus myself, and re-panel the wall. He eyed me with the look of one who had had to rectify the mistakes of DIY enthusiasts in the past, but agreed to quote on that basis. Having begrudgingly accepted that this office Walla had deprived him of some business, he advised me in an avuncular fashion that I should not do the re-panelling until the wall had dried thoroughly and we could see that the infestation had died. This might take a month.

I purchased a face mask and a pack of plastic sacks and set about the foul task of purifying the abysmal courtyard. The job took a whole day including a good scrubbing with disinfectant and trip to the local dump to dispose of the bulging sacks. These were the days of "totters". As soon as a car approached the elevated ramp above the rubbish skips, men who looked as if they were straight out of a Dickens' novel, scurried up ladders and into the containers, (which were unlabeled and did not require rubbish to be sorted), to inspect the goods which had been deposited there. Anything of metal scrap value or items in a possibly repairable state were recovered and added to a mound of paraphernalia of every description. My load when cast down from the trailer to the skip was, to say the least, a disappointment to them.

We moved the office temporarily into the room across the corridor and set about adding to the damage already done by the surveyor by ripping out the remaining panels. This left us with a pile of contaminated, splintered wood to get rid of. We considered various ruses to circumvent the Council requirement that we should not remove the wood from the building and potentially cause the rest of the City to be visited by this plague.

One option was to saw the pile into small pieces, seal the result into plastic sacks and take it to our garden at home to burn. This idea was quickly discarded when Hazel suggested that if the wood was to be cut into small pieces then we might just as well burn it in the office fireplace. Like all buildings of the era before central heating, every room at the School had a fireplace.

We rolled up the newly fitted carpet and together we cut the wood into relatively small chunks. Hazel volunteered to feed and tend to the fire which we had lit in the grate. I continued with the teaching of our one one-to-one corporate student in a classroom on the first floor and Barbro was about her business in our temporary office. Thus we were able to give a semblance of normality to the world while our problem panelling was disposed of.

It was our custom to join students at break time for a cup of coffee in the student lounge which was, as already described, on the ground floor next to the currently defunct office. So, thus it was that Barbro and I were sitting enjoying a cup with our student when I became aware that the smell of burning was in some way permeating through to the room we were in. Initially it was slight and merited a comment and an explanation to the student, but as we sat there trying to ignore it, the odiferous nuisance became increasingly embarrassing. I decided to go in and have a word with our stoker to see how long this situation would pertain.

Hazel was kneeling beside the fireplace her ash be-smudged face reddened by the intensity of the blaze and her dress clearly showing the signs of her current occupation with many sooty marks. But most alarming of all was the fact that smoke was curling up though the gaps in the floorboards and filling the room to the extent that it would soon be impossible to see her, let alone for her to breath. But why was the smoke coming through the floorboards?

I rushed down to the cellar and to my horror found that the metal fire basket from the grate above was now nestling in a pile of several discarded cardboard boxes once used to transport our goods to the building. They were well alight. I realised that to try to get them into the street through the subterranean door would allow air in to feed the fire. Worse still the floorboards above my head were beginning to burn.

I moved at a speed that only a man with fire at his heels could do and ran up and into the kitchen to get a bucketful of water. With this I managed to extinguish Hazel's inferno in the office fireplace and then after quickly explaining to Barbro that it might be prudent for her to take a stroll outside with the one-to-one student, Hazel and I poured further buckets of water through the hole which had appeared in the floor where the fire basket had made its exit and soaked the smouldering floorboards. By dint of feverish stamping I was able to put out the conflagration in the cellar.

We were left with a very smelly school, a hole in the floor of the office and pile of contaminated wood which had only diminished by half. But, fortunately we still had a building. Apparently, and clearly unobserved by us, the fire bricks under the grate had been removed at some time in the house's history and the fire we had lit in the metal basket had bare floorboards underneath and not fire-proof bricks!

After this episode I had no compunction about delivering the remaining despoiled panelling for the inspection of the totters.

The builders quickly came to do their work. At that time, the UK was in a deep recession and builders, like many other trades, were readily available without the inevitable delays experienced in economic boom times.

The weeks passed, but although I had tried to remove the creeping white web, the dry rot showed no sign of diminishing in its effort to take over the world. The damp course was now in place and the possibility of water rising through the brickwork was excluded, yet the fungus flourished. Another annoying factor was that although I had cleansed the courtyard the number of roosting pigeons seemed if anything to have increased in number, perhaps on account of me providing a more wholesome environment for them.

I decided that at least I could do something about this latter menace. I purchased some stout netting and squeezed the ladder through my office and out into the courtyard to put a net ceiling in place to thwart the guano gang. It was while wiring up the net against the office wall that I happened to grab the antediluvian down pipe for support. Part of it came away off the wall in my right hand. Fortunately, I had a firm grip on the ladder with my other hand and I held onto the down pipe. I immediately noticed that there was a rusty hole at the back of the pipe which could not be seen from the front when it was in position. Inspection of the wall behind where the pipe had been, showed that it was stained by water. Here was the source of the damp! My joy was somewhat tempered by the thought that we had just paid over £300 to the builders for a job which was obviously unnecessary. Perhaps it was here that the seeds were sown which, through my professional life, gave me an increasingly cynical view of the opinions of "experts".

Having replaced the down pipe, our fungus first retreated and then dried up. The work of rebuilding the panelling and repairing our scorched floorboards done, we moved back into the main office before Christmas 1980.

One other occurrence worthy of note was that on 25th November, at 1400 I had a visit from a Mr Hobley, of Her Majesty's Customs and Excise. This was our first VAT inspection and an event I had been dreading. I should hasten to add, that as far as I was aware, all our financial dealings had been of the utmost propriety….except one. I was in some terror of this event, partly because I was doing all the bookkeeping myself and although I had assiduously read "Teach Yourself Accounting", I had no previous experience whatever of running accounts. It should be noted here that these were pre-computer days and accounts were frequently, like mine, done in pen on a ledger. This inspection was to be the acid test of the efficacy of my self-taught skill. However, my greatest fear was generated by the odd transaction forced upon me by our solicitor. It will be remembered that he had done the legal work on the lease for the building and had requested a "special" arrangement in the settlement of his fees. He had requested that I should purchase a large quantity of tiles for the kitchen of his cottage in Dorset in lieu of paying against an invoice. He assured me that this arrangement was "normal" and would be much cheaper for us. To me it seemed unusual, very odd even, but since I was new to doing business in the UK and this man was an advocate after all, I went along with the ploy.

I duly noted the purchase in my accounts, but of course such a record in the ledger did not state who the tiles were for. What I had to face now was the awful possibility that Mr Hobley, if he was at all observant, would be quite likely to wonder why I had bought 300 kitchen tiles when our kitchen was only six feet by ten and indeed there were no tiles on the wall.

I left the accounts with him in the classroom next to my office and awaited the dreaded call to explain myself. After what seemed an eternity I decided that his claws might be blunted by the offer of a cup of tea. I went into the classroom without knocking and took him totally by surprise. My accounts were in a neat pile on the table alongside his feet. In his hands he held a copy of the Times, much crumpled by action of trying to make it invisible to me. He quickly took his feet off the table and pushed his paper into his open briefcase beside him. "Ah yes, Mr Wills everything seems to be in order and I will be on my way. I will call you at about the same time in a year's time to make another appointment". As a footnote to this matter of a lawyer putting me in such jeopardy, the house in Dorset which had been tiled at the school's expense and caused my extreme discomfort, later burned to the ground in mysterious circumstances and rumour has it that the lawyer fled to Northern Cyprus.

It had been an eventful year. We now had premises to be proud of and a few satisfied company contacts, despite almost cremating one of their employees. Our customer contact network was growing, albeit slowly. We needed a break to spend some time with the children and had hoped to visit my in-laws to celebrate Christmas, but I really could not justify denuding our pitiful capital by travelling with the whole family.

Some initiative was called for. I had, in the past, made an expensive venture possible in impecunious times by using a little imagination. When Barbro and I married in 1970, we had spent all our funds on buying our first house and short of going on a camping holiday, which would not have been too romantic in March, we could not afford a honeymoon. So I had publicised among my students the possibility of a group trip to England with Barbro, me and two of our very good teacher friends, Janet Wise and Rolf Meyer, as leaders. At that time the pound was at about its lowest rate ever against the krona and shopping in England was much in vogue for Swedes. The response was overwhelming from students, most of whom were older and did not have the confidence to travel to England alone. We had to limit the number of travellers to forty two so that we could use one coach to and from airports. And so it was, that we had a honeymoon in England, albeit in the company of forty two dependents, and even made a profit.

To solve the financial dilemma this time I contacted branches of the Swedish educational trust to see if any English departments needed books from England for the start of the new term in 1981. I received two substantial orders. I intended to use the profit from these orders and the money which would have been the cost of freight for the books, to finance our Christmas journey, which would include visits to potential clients. I planned to take the books with us. I had a trailer which I had used over a period of three years and sixteen journeys to transport all our goods to England before our move.

And so ended our first year as language school proprietors, but not before one further twist to add to our new life's rich canvas. I had carefully researched the requirements of the Swedish customs authorities regarding the import of teaching materials and acquired all the necessary forms. Completing them was onerous, but necessary to ensure easy clearance on arrival at Gothenburg. No duty was payable on teaching materials but VAT was due on the whole consignment. I worked out the amount payable and took my Swedish cheque book with me to pay the cost of this.

We arrived at a snowy Gothenburg harbour in the afternoon of the Sunday before Christmas. Knowing that I had been meticulous about the customs declaration, I had taken the seemingly minimal risk of buying one extra bottle of brandy over our normal allowance to contribute to my father-in-law's drinks cabinet, being fully aware of the exorbitant cost of spirits in Sweden. I had hidden this "extra" bottle under my driver's seat.

Brimming with confidence born of my careful preparations, I drove up to the customs post and proffered the forms to one of the two officers already eying my trailer with undisguised excitement. He took the form and went inside to the comfort of his office to study it for imperfections. The other officer asked me to uncover the trailer and to allow the contents to be inspected. Afterwards the two of them conferred and with an air of disappointment, agreed that the papers were in order and accurately described the consignment. I was presented with an invoice denoting the amount to be paid in VAT. I started to write a cheque when in unison they asked what I was doing and when told, as if rehearsed, in chorus they said, "The customs does not accept cheques!"

"But then how do people pay?" I asked lamely.

"You must have an account with a shipping agent or pay cash".

This was long before the days when you could obtain cash from ATM machines at any time of the day or night, so we were at an impasse. I had three children and a wife getting colder by the minute now that our car engine had been turned off and a long dark and icy drive ahead of me, which I wanted to get started on before the snow got much worse. I debated the options with the two officers who by now had been joined by a second pair, they having cleared all the other vehicles disembarked from the ferry. It seemed that my only option was to leave the trailer at the docks overnight. We would then have to stay in Gothenburg and get cash the next morning to retrieve our trailer and get the thousands of pounds worth of books out of hock. This solution was going to be expensive for us and extremely disappointing for the children who were so excited about seeing their Swedish grandparents. It was also complicated by the fact that I had a large proportion of the books in the back of the car and our lighter luggage in the trailer to better balance the load. It would mean completely repacking.

Then one of the quartet of our tormentors suggested that there might be another solution. There was a bank at Gothenburg airport which was open at weekends. Gothenburg airport, then Torslanda, was about thirty minutes from the harbour. Hugely relieved by this glimmer of hope I suggested that I leave the trailer at the harbour and drive to the airport to cash a cheque. Oh no! This was too much for the quartet. Clearly, we looked altogether too devious to be entrusted with such a mission. I was required to leave Barbro and the children and the trailer with the customs as a guarantee that I would return. But even this was not enough to satisfy their fear that I would abandon my family and go on the run. An officer must accompany me to the airport!

At least Barbro and the children were allowed to go into the warmth of the customs office during my absence. I drove off with my new companion and as we rounded the gate at the harbour entrance I heard a faint clink under my seat. It was the brandy bottle! The bottle was rolling from side to side as I turned corners. As we drove through the town each corner presented a new risk that my guilty secret would be revealed and that an already fraught situation would be made seriously worse. I explained that I was very nervous about driving on icy roads and took each corner at a speed which reflected such a level of caution that I feared that my mobile jailer's suspicions might be awoken. As we approached the airport I began to wonder how to get the officer out of the car while I was in the terminal building so that he might not investigate the source of the clinking. I was hugely relieved when he insisted on accompanying me to the bank and back.

It was thus, after returning to the harbour, paying the cash and hitching the trailer, and in a state of near nervous exhaustion, we started on the six hour drive to Uppsala and eventually to a joyful midnight reunion with my mother- and father-in-law, Elsa and Bjorn. My adage that there is no such thing as an easy honest profit in business was ringing in my ears like the Christmas bells. No gain without pain. The brandy tasted good but marked the end of my smuggling career.

Chapter 3   1981 Things start to take shape

Safely back in England we re-opened the School in the second week of January. A fanfare was not necessary as there was no one there to hear it. But by the third week we had three or four au pairs studying together part-time, though paying a desultory fee for doing so. However, people make people and we needed the School to be alive and for the word to get around.

We soon had two adult group course students studying together, Marianne from Sweden and Elba from Ecuador. At this stage I was getting more applications from prospective teachers than from students. On 17th January I interviewed another International House London, teacher, Barbara Hickman, who had recently moved to Salisbury. I was also becoming aware that there were many talented EFL teachers available locally who I would like to have employed if we had had work for them. This fact dogged me for most of my time at the school. Apart from the busiest time of the year, the summer, I had the constant dilemma of trying to find enough work to satisfy the earning needs of some really gifted teachers in order to deserve and preserve their loyalty. The work flow was never constant and we had no way of controlling the variations especially since the most teacher intensive activity, one-to-one teaching was very sporadic. Also, our programme of special courses meant that some weeks we needed twice or more times the number of teachers we might require the following weeks. I really felt sorry and almost ashamed when I had to tell staff that we would not be able to offer them work the following week or longer. But in the main, teachers could see that we were fighting to survive and grow and that teacher requirement was student led.

As Barbro would be busy teaching on the Swedish courses, in February we employed an office assistant, Sheila Pink, the wife of an Air Force officer, to work half time. The first course took place that month and was very successful. It was interesting for me to meet the "English end" of Swedish companies. The participants were highly motivated, but some were very impatient learners and got quite exasperated by the time and effort required to acquire and retain new language. One of them, J.D. had learnt some Swedish from a pre-war Linguaphone course and caused much merriment when he came out with antiquated phrases in Swedish such as "please brush my bowler hat" or "I need a room for my man".

We ran two of these courses in February, one in May and two follow-up courses in September. The pressure on Barbro was immense as she was the only teacher on the courses and also ran a correspondence course which she had written for students to maintain their language skills between courses. However, the revenue was extremely important for us and was certainly much better than we had yet earned from our English courses!

During the spring we ran the first of our English courses for nurse tutors. These were really enjoyable for the staff with highly motivated, personable students. Part of the courses involved study visits to hospitals and doctors surgeries. Arranging these required me to interface with the local community much more than previously. A spin off from this was that the School began to get recognition and some standing in the area.

The only downside of these courses, and we had five or six of them over a period of two years, was what I can only describe as a totally out of character stinginess at social events. Barbro and I always had a meal with the students at the end of their course. A great time was had by all and there was usually some interaction with the locals as a group of twenty or so Swedish females generally attracted some attention in the pub. However, when it came to settling the bill it was dreadful.

Comments such as "I should pay less because I only had half a glass of wine", or "You should pay part of the cost of my extra chips as you had some of them", soured the end of the evening. These disputes became an expected and unavoidable ritual after these events which usually ended up with me paying the disputed amounts to defuse the situation.

In the spring Nick McIver declared himself homeless and asked if he could move into one of the unused rooms in the attic until he could find permanent accommodation. Hazel announced herself willing to share the ancient bathroom and so we tidied up another of the rooms for him.

Shortly before Easter a past Swedish colleague of mine contacted me to tell me that her best friend, who was training manager at a large pharmaceutical company in Uppsala, was looking for a school in England to be their main supplier for one-to-one (private), lessons for lower and middle management employees. The company, at that time called Fortia (subsequently called Pharmacia), was substantial in size and had a very generous training budget. This was a fantastic opportunity for us but we were up against a number of very well established schools in cities which were much better known as EFL centres and perceived to have more attraction than Salisbury, so I decided to visit the company to make our case.

I was invited to visit the training manager, Eva Wallin. She agreed to send a manager from the Personnel Department, Bo Soderlund, as a guinea pig for a one week course from 30th March. We drew up a plan for a succession of employees, sometimes up to three at a time, to go to Salisbury for one or two weeks study, subject to this and subsequent courses being successful. The downside was that the company expected a very low introductory price for the first year. I realised that the only way to get a foot in would be to offer a price they could not refuse. We agreed on £5 per lesson of 45 minutes during this trial period.

This contact was to turn out to be pure gold for us as not only did we later discover that Pharmacia had an English language training requirement in some of its overseas subsidiaries but our contact in the Uppsala training department was to eventually recommend us to her fellow training managers in three other major Swedish companies. The short term problem for our cash-strapped school with these courses was that because of the low introductory price it was only when I myself was teaching that we actually made any money. Obviously, we had every intention to raise the price the following year.

Despite our good fortune with Fortia and with the Swedish courses it was clear that we would need to make a lot of money in the summer to keep the business going through the winter. It was also clear from our first one-to-one student evaluations that we would have to do something about our decrepit heating system.

In April, Nick McIver asked if we would consider running a summer teenagers' course for an Italian teacher friend of his, Carlo Sigismondi. Desperate situations require desperate measures! We agreed.

And so it was, that we ran our first young learners' course. I hesitate to say that we compromised our principles rather that we bowed to the inevitable. We had to increase revenue and we were looking a gift horse in the mouth. What we did decide, was that teenagers' courses would be kept physically separate from adult courses by running them in a different building. This is a principle which we adhered to for twenty five years. While this might be considered a questionable business decision as the school building was more than half empty, we determined not to mix adults and children in the same premises, and to accept the consequent expense.

However, finding another building was not easy. State schools did not break up until the third week in July and our summer course would start in the first week of the month. There was another issue which thankfully was solved when State schools were eventually given responsibility for their own finances. Until that time, any rent generated by letting school buildings did not benefit the school in question but went to the County Council. This meant that in our early years there was no motivating factor to make a school go to the inconvenience of letting rooms to us. Later on when the proceeds of lettings went directly to the school's coffers, we developed a very good relationship with several State schools, in particular South Wilts Girl's Grammar School where we were able to rent classrooms even when their own school was in session.

In 1981, the only place we could find for our fledgling teenage summer school was St Edmund's Church Hall. This was conveniently situated five minutes from the main school. The Hall was not the cheeriest of places. The caretaker, Mr N. was an avuncular pipe smoking gent. It was clear that we were in his thrall when we were using the rooms. Everything had to be done his way and only after some considerable persuasion could we arrange chairs in a semi circle instead of in rows. And oh yes, the chairs! There was a core stock of steel rimmed canvas covered chairs which, to judge by the stretching and fading had seen sterling service under some very sturdy backsides for a considerable number of years. These were mixed with a collection of venerable wooden chairs of varying degrees of comfort and states of repair, the majority of which had probably been unsold items in jumble sales held on the premises over many decades. Nothing but nothing, could persuade the caretaker to try to furnish the rooms uniformly or to dispose of items of furniture which were damaged or unsightly.

However, although we avoided using the Hall as much as possible in later years, and then when we did it was mainly for social events, on the occasions we had bookings we often wished that Mr N was still in charge as he was replaced by an ex-policeman, Mr D., who definitely did not like the Hall to be used at all and certainly not by foreigners. He expected us to clean and furnish the Hall each time we used it and displayed a distinct lack of charm when dealing with our staff.

And so the summer of 1981 hove into view, but not before we ran a course for another new client, Uppsala University. A very good friend, Richard Glover, one of the most talented pedagogues I have ever had the pleasure to work with, was a lecturer at the university and had been asked to arrange a two-week course in England for students from his faculty. In May, thirty of his students livened things up for us. This was a precursor to what was, relatively speaking, a lively time in July.

With the confidence born of this increase in activity in the spring, I asked for quotes to install central heating on the ground and first floors. The best price was £3000. I arranged for a meeting on the 30th July with Mr Matthews, the Manager of our bank, National Westminster. I presented my business plan and asked for a loan of £3000. On the 8th July I received a letter refusing to lend us the money. This led us to move our bank to Lloyds. In later years, when our turnover was near two million pounds, I had enormous pleasure when National Westminster came a courting us, to remind them of the reason we moved to Lloyds.

Eventually, we solved the difficulty of financing the central heating by asking the landlord to pay for the installation and to raise the rent commensurately.

And so the time came for the arrival of our first group of Young Learners at the beginning of July. The Italians were to be with us for three weeks and staying with host families, two students to a family.

At that time there were no "no frills" airlines. Group leaders who were keen to maximise their profit, (or as was definitely the case with Carlo Sigismondi, to keep the cost of the trip down as low as possible so that even the children of less well-off parents could aspire to travel), chose charter flights. Experience was soon to show us that the more inconvenient the flight time, the cheaper the flight, and consequently the greater the likelihood that our clients would choose it.

We also had yet to learn about the certainty that the cheaper the transport we hired, the more likely the coach drivers were to be surly and have the welcoming charm of a rampant crocodile. More obvious was it that their coaches had seen better days and those days were lost somewhere in the mists of time. The quality and safety standards set by the authorities have changed dramatically in thirty years. We chose a company called Coombe Hill Coaches, but I will not divert the reader from the main track of this narrative by an exposé of coaching horror stories.

I met the driver at the coach park at 16.30 on the Sunday afternoon and we proceeded with much rattling, grinding of gears and driver's oaths directed at any motorist who impeded our progress, to Gatwick Airport. The construction of the southern M25 was not complete until 1985 and so the journey to Gatwick usually entailed leaving the M3 at Guildford and then driving across country on slow roads to Gatwick. This in turn meant that it was necessary to have a good time margin for journeys to allow for possible traffic hold-ups. Carlo's flight was landing at 20.00.

Once at the airport, I left the coach to park and hurried to the terminal to have some refreshment before the flight landed. I need not have hurried. The Arrivals board showed a ladder of "Delayed" notices. Our flight was delayed to 22.00. I joined the queue at the information desk to find the reason for the delay. Clearly, by the look on their faces, others had a similar mission. The queue edged forward and eventually it was my turn to address the tired-looking bearer of dismal news. She told me that the outgoing plane from Gatwick to Milan, Malpensa Airport had only just taken off.

In 1981 Gatwick Airport was a fairly basic place to spend an evening. One of the facilities which did not exist then, was an arrivals display board in the coach park to inform drivers about delays. So I trudged back to the park to give the glad tidings to our lugubrious driver. Surprisingly, he did not seem to be overly concerned. I learnt later when I received the bill for the transfer that the driver was on an enhanced hourly rate after midnight.

More problematic was the fact that host families would be expecting to gather at the School at 22.30 to meet their students. I phoned Barbro and told her the news. She called families to inform them that the earliest we could expect the group to arrive in Salisbury would be at 00.30, this time to be confirmed later.

At Gatwick the information display rattled each time news came through. "Delay 22.30". "Delay 23.15" and then at last "Expected 23.45". I woke the coach driver who was asleep on the back bench seat in his coach to give him the news. He was less than elated but relieved his grumpiness by reminding me that he had told me in Salisbury that charter flights are always late.

Back at the terminal I phoned Barbro. Now she had a real dilemma. She was very wary of the reaction she would get from families when they were asked to pick up their students at around 03.00. She pleaded with me to ask the coach driver to deliver the students to the accommodation addresses. In later years, hardened by this type of experience, but also with the confidence borne out of becoming friends with many of the host families, Barbro would not flinch at requesting a host family's attendance at Salisbury's dismal coach park at whatever time was necessary.

At half past midnight I found myself holding aloft my sign with the School's name among a group of others similarly engaged in meeting arrivals. I had already noticed the signs of some other language schools, but what perplexed me was the somewhat timid and unwelcoming attitude of the bearers of some signs. The signs themselves ranged from one drawn with a felt pen on the back of what could have been an envelope, to gaudy placards. Right then and there I coined the motto which our couriers would have drilled into them for years – "You only have one chance to make a first impression."

After waving my sign at numbers of passengers who did not react at all and were clearly destined for other places, I found myself facing a short athletic looking dynamo of a man who, grinning from ear to ear seized my outstretched hand and bellowed "Mike? I'm Carlo."

He was one of those men who have the perpetual stubble of someone who has not shaved for two days. It was never longer and never shorter; somehow he must have had the technique of shaving to leave this constant length. His dark eyes flashed behind John Lennon style glasses and his short black hair was so perfectly curled that it looked as if he must sleep with curlers in.

A noisy gaggle of boys and girls in much more colourful clothes than their English counterparts might have worn, clustered excitedly behind him. He apologised profusely for his late arrival, as if he had delayed the plane himself.

I led the group to the coach which, fortunately, had moved to the collection point, and proceeded to act as a buffer between the irascible driver and the students as they took their suitcases to the luggage boot. Then the driver heaved and pushed the cases into the void, cussing the size of them, but it soon became clear that thirty students' bags would not fit into a 45 seat coach baggage compartment. The driver pushed his way through the throng, went inside the coach and unceremoniously cleared those sitting on the back seat in order to open the emergency door. Carlo and I handed the remainder of the cases up for him to stack on the back seats. At last when all the packing was done, I dashed into the terminal to phone Barbro to say that we were just leaving. I then exhausted the driver's last iota of goodwill by telling him not to stop on the return journey, thus depriving him of his free service station meal.

Neither the students nor Carlo showed any sign of tiredness on the three hour drive. He chatted incessantly the entire way while I tried to work out from my badly lit map the order in which we should distribute the students. I had of course overlooked the fact that the suitcases were packed in no particular order and there was just no chance that they could be retrieved in the order in which we would deliver the students. The logical place to start dropping students was the suburb of Laverstock which was nearest to our entry point to the City and where eight or ten students were staying. We reached there at around 03.00. Need I describe the exasperation of the driver when he had to pull out most of the cases at each family address, in order to recover the two we required? Nor was it made easier by the fact that none of us had a torch.

However, it was Barbro who had visited the families and not me. I was totally unfamiliar with the area. Barbro could not have come to meet us at this hour as she could not abandon the children at home. And thus it was that I found myself searching for street names and even worse, house numbers. The reader might ask, why not just count the houses from the first to find the right numbers, this is fine in principle but often house numbers had "A"s or "B"s and in some cases the houses were in groups in no identifiable order. It seemed that the folk of Salisbury had conspired to make it as difficult as possible to identify house numbers. Some were on gates, some painted on porches and at best they were in raised figures on the front doors.

Since the coach could not drive down the neat cul-de-sacs and crescents, I had to leave the coach with its engine throbbing at what seemed a thunderous audio level, the students explaining which was their case like excited football supporters and the driver's occasional expletives echoing through the still of the night, while I tried to locate the correct house. Here and there I had to feel the numbers and read them Braille-like in order to identify the correct address. On one occasion I walked up some stone steps and having established that it was the wrong house I turned and tripped on the milk bottles. They bounced tunefully down the steps gathering momentum and volume before there was a tinkling crash as they met their fate on the path.

I had learnt after the first successful locating of a family, not to take the students with me as I skulked with seemingly villainous intent to find the right house. Their noisy excitement and even the rumbling of the suitcase wheels on the pavement had a dramatic effect on every dog in the neighbourhood.

Thankfully, some families had left a light on in the house and this eased matters considerably, except in the house where they had left the light on by mistake when they went to bed.

We proceeded around the town, each drop making it easier to find the student's suitcase amongst the jumble in the hold as the numbers diminished. Things were looking good until we turned a tight corner in Bellevue Road. Just around the corner, out of sight of the driver and unlit, road workers had parked a large two wheeled compressor, the type used for pneumatic drills. The driver tried to stop, but could not before there was a loud grinding noise and the coach was wedged up against the compressor. The students were treated to a verbal outburst as the driver accessed his store of strongest invective and he got out to survey the damage. Carlo proved not to be beyond manual labour as the three of us and several boys dragged the offending machine on to the pavement and away from the bus. At 05.15, having delivered the last of the students, I put Carlo's luggage in my car which was parked in Salt Lane car park and drove him to his home. There was no point in driving home, so, not for the last time, I got a couple of hours sleep on the floor of my office under my desk, (the darkest place in the room).

This transfer was an ordeal, but it was rich in lessons for the future. Over the next twenty six years we arranged over two thousand transfers and while each presented its own challenges, the mishaps of this first one shaped our policies and routines like none other.

On Monday morning, having had two hours sleep, we were at the School front door to greet our young guests as they were delivered to the School by their host families. It is, incidentally, an indication of the remarkable rise in prosperity in the City or perhaps the whole country, over the last thirty years, to note the mode of transport used by host families to ferry their guests to School on their first day. Nowadays, almost all students would be dropped off in relatively new, often second family cars. In 1981 most of the students would be walked to School or brought on the bus. Just a few being dropped off in vehicles which had seen better days. The notable exception being the family which thrilled their students, by driving them in their Rolls Royce. In fact, delivering the students on foot was much more useful to us as there was a better chance of the students getting to familiarize themselves with the town.

We like to think that the School contributed to this increased prosperity in the City. Over a period of twenty seven years we spent at least seven million pounds on family accommodation, money that went directly into the City's economy. In addition to this, a similar sum went on salaries and buying local services.

Once all the students were accounted for they were taken to St Edmund's House for their induction and testing before the classes got under way. I will not dwell in detail on the course, but here just reflect that many lessons were learnt by us, the organizers, especially concerning the importance of the out of school activities and student safety. As regards the latter, although of course we were concerned about the welfare and safety of our adult students, we had never been in the position before of having to consider every aspect of the care and security of vulnerable young people.

The out of school activities programme was our first attempt to interest and occupy teenagers of both exuberant and lethargic persuasions and it was not particularly successful. We did not have enough activities and those we had were just not good enough to engage all the students. Fortunately for us, Carlo was hugely energetic and could compensate for shortcomings on our part by finding extra activities for his students.

As I relate in the chapter on Social Activities, Salisbury just did not have enough recreational activities to offer young people and so we eventually had to create our own arsenal of social and sporting diversions.

Having said this, with good leadership and well intentioned students, a lot can be done with a little. Show an Italian or Spanish group of teenagers a green space and give them a ball and they will immediately sort themselves into players and admirers and occupy themselves happily for a good while.

As regards leadership, this is a prime factor which impacts heavily on the success or otherwise of a course. The leaders are usually teachers or representatives of the agency sending the group. We saw an extraordinary range of people doing this job. They varied from incredibly caring, excellent organisers to scoundrels who exploited their students financially and in one case we have good reason to believe, sexually.

There were those who could even turn all manner of adverse occurrences such as bad weather or a major traffic jam delaying an excursion, into a positive experience for the students. But there were also some whose negative attitudes or fussiness presented us with major challenges. There were prima donnas, perverts, skinflints and one or two lacking confidence so badly that we had to allocate staff "minders" for them. Some haunted the school all day demanding huge amounts of staff time while others just disappeared to the shops as soon as the students had been handed over to our care. One female Mexican leader even abandoned her group altogether and eloped with a Swedish adult student. However, the vast majority were caring, responsible individuals who made our job much, much easier. Carlo, as I have mentioned was one of those at the very top end of the quality scale.

Carlo liked the City, he appreciated the fact that we had a serious approach to education and that our teachers were well trained and professional and we were not long into the course before he was talking about coming next year with a bigger group. This was music to our ears because we were actually enjoying having these young people around and of course we needed the business.

The strength of our organisation was of paramount importance to us and despite the shortcomings in this the first of our Young Learners' courses we were now keen to develop this new branch of our activities. We had a new recognition that the four elements of a successful course for teenagers were accommodation, security, out of school activities and the teaching programme and that the first two were paramount. Clients had to have absolute confidence about these two elements before even deciding whether the rest of the package was worth considering.

The complexity of planning such courses appealed to both Barbro and me and eventually our eldest daughter Anna, also showed considerable talent in this. I am certain that careful planning of every aspect of our operations contributed greatly to our survival and the enhancement of our reputation. However, we also recognised increasingly that though through thorough planning the "expected" can be managed; it is the "unexpected" which really tests an organisation's mettle. And neither does experience of dealing with the unforeseen totally safeguard against nasty surprises, for even after twenty five years we often reflected that just when you think you have seen it all there is still a surprise waiting around the corner! This is the consequence of working in a "people" industry.

Of course other things were happening during the summer in the main School building. We had a number of one-to-one students, a small number of adults studying in groups but most of the students were teachers on our teachers' refresher courses. In all we ran 5 of these courses in the summer.

Both Ann and Nick were kept busy with these and they proved to be very successful. For my part, I was so busy with the planning and organisation that I rarely had a chance to teach during the summer. It gradually dawned on me that if the organisation was to grow then my role was going to be increasingly desk-bound, at least in the summer time.

The latter was brought home to me one day when I had been sitting most of the day catching up with the book-keeping and preparing the VAT return. I became aware of music coming from upstairs. This was not unusual; the teacher trainers often used recorded music. But this was live music with Nick playing his guitar and singing. How I wished that I could have been in that classroom!

As an adult I have been lucky enough to have a modicum of musical ability and a loud if not perfect baritone register. Music has opened many doors for me. I do not really remember when I started playing the guitar; I guess that it was around the age of 15 when Bill Kittle lent me a ¾ size pearl inlaid guitar, a family heirloom belonging to his aunt, so that I could join his skiffle group. I do remember vividly the reluctance with which I returned it to him when the group members went their separate ways.

When I started my teacher training, flushed with the funds from my grant cheque, I bought my own guitar. The level of social acceptance in my all male college, St Peter's College, Birmingham, hinged on a range of factors by which the individual was judged by his peers. These included the perceived or convincingly lied about abilities to drink prodigious amounts of beer, bed women at will, excel on the sports field or leave all exam revision until the night before the exam and yet pass. Secondary factors included a facility to tell lewd jokes or play a musical instrument. Since in my second year I was elected Chairman of the Social and Entertainments Committee, (and thus qualified for superior in-college accommodation), I assume that my ability to sing and play the guitar must have compensated for weaknesses in other areas.

In the early sixties the burgeoning music scene presented many opportunities to make money with the guitar. I was lucky enough to get holiday work as a minor entertainer, but when two good friends decided to give up College to go professional I decided not to join them. This was one of the better decisions in my life though subsequently seeing my chums on TV, before they disappeared into oblivion, did give me fleeting regrets.

Financially, the summer of 1981 should have given us a breathing space to develop our year-round activities. However, here I had a harsh lesson in cash-flow budgeting. The size of our immediate post-summer bank balance lured me into investing too heavily in replacing our aging classroom furniture, much of which had been bought second-hand, and buying office- and classroom equipment. By October I realised that in financial terms this had been foolishly precipitous. I had no overdraft facility and no possibility of a business loan. We were once again living on our savings and such current income as we had. Things were precarious and we were still in a position where the company could not afford to pay me a salary and that paid to Barbro was fairly derisory.

We had a sporadic but important flow of one-to-one students through the autumn and a few group adult students. I started an audio recorded monthly UK news programme which we offered for sale on subscription to one-to-one students and to those on teachers' courses to give them the opportunity of maintaining their listening skills after they had returned to their own countries. This was called "The Month In Britain". At first, I wrote the manuscripts and recorded the master tape at home and duplicated the tapes by collecting all the classroom cassette recorders one evening each month and connecting them together to mass produce the students cassettes. It gave a useful but small financial contribution to the organisation. But overall our profitability level was very low. Paraphrasing the words of Mr Macawber, "Something had to turn up". And it did.

In 1965 I had had the great good fortune to be selected for a post as an English teacher with the British Centre in Sweden. The Centre was a branch of the large educational trust which I mentioned earlier. Each year around sixty UK teachers were recruited to join the teaching staff of well over a hundred, who were working in towns and cities all over Sweden. The reason that there was a considerable turnover of teachers was that the Swedish government allowed tax-free status to UK teachers for a period of two years. If teachers stayed for a third year, they had to pay the income tax they would have paid for the first two years. In order to preserve some continuity and to staff senior positions within the organisation, the Centre paid the income tax for a very small number of teachers to stay on for a third and further years.

For someone with an interest in education and an eye to the main chance, Sweden in the mid-sixties was the right place at the right time. Generous funding was available for students to learn and for language teachers to develop materials and methodology. This was facilitated by the buoyant post-war Swedish economy and driven by the political realisation that Sweden was a small country which needed to trade and involve itself internationally in order to prosper. Only since the war had English become the first foreign language in schools. There was a whole generation over the age of thirty which had learned German as their only or main foreign language.

The British Centre was one of several state and local community financed organisations charged with giving this generation the opportunity to learn English. These organisations were in competition with each other. The Centre's unique selling point was that all of their teachers were what was termed "trained native English speakers". Each August there was a four week EFL training course in Stockholm for the new intake of teachers which culminated in a week's teaching practice. After this, teachers were posted to their town of appointment. There was an air of mystery until the end of the course over where each teacher was to be posted and then on the penultimate day of the course the appointments would be announced by an extraordinary woman called Anne- Marie Lundberg. She had a prodigious work capacity and a memory which seemed to include all the names and towns of appointment of teachers over the last fifteen years. In addition she was a very pleasant person and a great character, who was later to become a close friend.

I was sent to the town of Falun in the province of Dalarna. In the subsequent year I moved to Uppsala and I was fortunate enough to be offered a third year contract. Eventually, on the retirement of the Head of the organisation, Ian Dunlop, I was appointed Director of Teacher Training and Development in Stockholm working under Anne-Marie. My responsibilities included teaching quality control, teacher training and joint responsibility with Anne-Marie for teacher recruitment. The latter was to an extent delegated to Michael Lewis, an ex-teacher who was based in the UK recruitment office in Brighton. In addition to a major intake of teachers each August, the organisation also recruited around twelve teachers each January. These teachers had a shorter training course as they were required to start teaching in late January.

In November 1981 I received a phone call from Anne-Marie in Stockholm to ask if I might be interested in taking over the British Centre teacher recruitment scheme as they had decided that since they wished to cut the cost of teacher recruitment they would like to close the Brighton office. This was a most welcome opportunity to work with my old colleague and importantly, to create a new revenue stream. We agreed that I should give a quote for the contract and that if this was acceptable we should meet in Stockholm on 21st December to finalise the agreement. So, in late December the family once more headed off to Sweden to celebrate Christmas. I managed visits to three of our corporate clients and then on the 21st December I visited Anne-Marie at the British Centre and finalised the agreement. The terms were that I would do all the advertising for teachers and take up references for suitable candidates. I would arrange a short list of candidates for interview by a panel from Sweden and me at various centres around the UK during each spring and autumn. Further, I would arrange briefing meetings for teachers appointed and run the training course in Salisbury in August and book transport to Sweden for the teachers and their baggage.

I was faced with a dilemma about what to call the recruitment organisation; I could not use the School's name as this would be misleading to potential applicants. On the advice of our accountants I set up a company called Salisbury International Language Services, (SILS), having ascertained that the recruitment of teachers was not liable for VAT. The thought of two VAT inspections on a regular basis was just too much. We had, by the by, had our second SSE inspection on 4th November and my homespun bookkeeping system was approved for the second time.

Thus ended another formative year for the School and through the British Centre contract I had at least one guarantee of income in the next!

Chapter 4   1982   After the fire the flood

The winter between 1981 and 1982 is memorable. The Christmas period had been cold, but on the 8th and 9th of January there were severe blizzards and the temperature plummeted. Throughout the snowfall, which lasted over 36 hours, temperatures were between -2 and -4C so the snow was dry and powdery and drifted freely in the wind. Transport services were completely dislocated over a wide area and millions of commuters failed to get to work in London two days running. South Wales was isolated for three days and troops were brought in to deliver essentials and to help clear roads.

Following the blizzard the cold tightened its grip. Early on the morning of the 10th January the temperature fell to -26.1C at Newport in Shropshire, breaking the record for England which had been set just four weeks earlier. In Scotland, Braemar recorded -27.2C on the same morning, equalling the UK's all-time record which had been set way back in 1895. As far south as Wiltshire, daytime maxima below -10C were recorded on the 13th, as freezing fog blanketed many areas.

We opened the School on Monday 11th January for a one-to-one student from Pharmacia, Bo Quarnstrom. Even our new heating system did not provide the comfort a Swede expected indoors, so we rigged up extra heaters to make him comfortable. Fortunately for us he was a reasonable individual who could understand that these were extreme circumstances. His course was for one week and despite the circumstances, it went well. The following week we had several adult group students starting and we were going to open two classes.

On Saturday the temperature rose considerably and a thaw set in. Unusually, we did not go into the School over the weekend and Hazel was not returning to take up residence for another week. So it was, that around eight o'clock on the morning of 18th January, Barbro and I arrived to open up. As soon as I opened the door I realised that something was very wrong, I could hear a noise inside although I was still in the little porch. I rushed in with Barbro behind me. Before us was a scene of devastation such as I would not like to see again. Water was pouring through the ceiling, parts of which had fallen down, on to sodden carpets. The new wallpaper was detached from the walls in some places and in others it was sagging and threatening to fall.

We splashed into the office and found water raining down on such equipment as we had and on documents left on the desks. I ran upstairs and found a similar scene of woe. The water was coming from the attic. I wrenched the swollen attic door open and ran upstairs. There, in the ancient bathroom was the source of the water flow. The cold water supply to the toilet had split wide open. I hunted around, by now wet through, trying to find a stop cock. There was none on the top floor, but I remembered that there was in the ground floor. I went down and turned it off. The flow from above slowly began to diminish.

Barbro and I waded around the ground floor trying to recover whatever papers and books we could find which were not water damaged and put them in the kitchen, one of two rooms on the ground floor which was undamaged. The other room which had not been affected was the student common room.

Upstairs two classrooms were relatively unscathed though there was an all pervading dampness in the building. We decided that our priority was to stay open and use the two class rooms and the common room for the students who would be attending class this week. We needed more help with the salvage operation; the teachers were needed in class so I called my parents who by then lived in Salisbury. They soon arrived with mops and buckets. I drove off to hire pumps to try to drain the cellar which now had the appearance of a Roman cistern. Once we had got the pumps going I contacted our insurers and then an emergency plumber. Fortunately, by mid-day we once more had a tamed water supply.

So what had happened? The attic had been unoccupied since before Christmas and although there was a small radiator which had been left on, it was clearly unable to provide enough heat to prevent the pipes in the bathroom from freezing. When the thaw set in, the pipes defrosted, and in so doing, split.

Our few students and two teachers were extremely supportive and we were able to keep the School open. We realised however, that it would be foolish to take any further bookings until we had put the building in order.

The damage was immense. Most of the building needed to be redecorated and, once the furniture had begun to dry out, tables and desks began to split. One casualty was a fine antique walnut pedestal table which was in my office. This was a family heirloom and we were particularly sad to see that it was severely damaged by the water.

It should be remembered that at that time all administration was paper based, there were no office computers. All of our records, host families, students, enquiries and financial accounts were in the water stained mess that was our office.

Despite frequent calls to our insurers we were unable to establish what we could claim for and if we could get builders and decorators in to put things top right. Eventually, on 12th February, an insurance loss adjuster, a Mr Hogben, turned up. After a tour of inspection of the building, which by this time had dried out, we sat down to discuss the situation. He fired the first salvo in the insurance company's effort to minimise my claim.

"Mr Wills, you realise that you are under insured", said he.

"But it was the local representative of the insurers who recommended the amount we should insure for."

This put him on the back foot but not for long.

"Have you acquired equipment and furniture since the insurance proposal was accepted?"

The fact was that we had, but not a great deal.

"So, Mr Wills, I'm sorry to have to tell you that your insurance claim will be subject to averaging. This means that the amount we will reimburse you will be lowered in proportion to what we assess your level of underinsurance to be."

He asked me for the inventory which I had made, together with an indication of the value of each item. At the end of the list I had put the walnut table but I had written, "Value unknown".

Mr Hogben glossed the list and then described to me how I should get two quotes from builders to repair the damage. They would pay only 90% of the cost of repairs because of the averaging.

"Mr Wills, I see that you have a Continuity Insurance."

I had no idea what this was but clearly we were paying for it so perhaps we could claim something.

"Has this incident caused you to lose any business or indeed will you need to close while repairs are taking place?"

Suddenly, Scrooge had become Father Christmas.

"Indeed, our business has been badly affected. We are not taking new enrolments or advertising for students at the moment and we will have to cancel our Easter courses."

"Would you give me a breakdown of how much business you have lost and the cost please?"

Now, how could I with my hand firmly on my heart, give an exact figure of business we might have had, had the School been fully operational? I have to admit that the figure I gave him was notional and perhaps erred slightly towards how much business we would like to have had.

As he was about to leave, Mr Hogben asked to see the walnut table. On seeing the sorry sight, far from agreeing that it was a write off, he examined it carefully.

"We can do something with this," he said. "I will send a furniture restorer to collect it."

Clearly, the table was more valuable than we had known as it was obviously cheaper to restore the table than to pay us its value.

We had had the fire and now we had had the flood. Both events tested our mettle and though both had really caused us to delve deep into our reserves of resilience they were character forming, they brought Barbro and me closer together and strengthened our resolve to make a success of this venture. They also prepared us for further, though by comparison minor, misadventures in the future.

Oh, and the table? It was returned to us by a magician of a furniture restorer in absolute pristine condition, far better than it had been before.

Chapter 5　　　　　　　We go on![1]

The School population was still very small and while this was not a good situation, it did mean that we got to know our students very well. We became real friends with some of them. I have mentioned Andrea Cecchi already. Two others I remember fondly are Helen and Peter Steiner from Switzerland. They came back, time after time, good customers and valued friends.

On 1st February, Jenny Forsberg and Anne-Marie Lundberg came from Stockholm to formalise the arrangements for the teacher recruitment scheme. I learnt, to my great pleasure and surprise that they required 65 new teachers for September 1982. We agreed that our first interview sessions, which they would attend, would be in London for three days from 19th March and subsequently for two days in Salisbury.

On the back of this contract, I was able to persuade our new bank, Lloyds, to give us an overdraft facility and on the 3rd March I met the manager, Chris Kedgeley, who agreed to let us have a maximum of £3000.

The interviews went well and we had three further sessions before gathering all the teachers appointed to briefing sessions in London, Edinburgh and Manchester. In those long off days, in order to work in Sweden it was necessary to apply for a labour permit at the Swedish Consulate in London. One of my duties was to arrange for this to be done. So, at each briefing session I collected in the teachers' passports for submission to the Consulate.

The last briefing session was in Manchester after which I had over sixty passports in my briefcase. At the airport I was stopped by airport security, quite an unusual thing in those days. They asked to see the contents of my briefcase. It took over an hour to persuade some very enthusiastic policemen that I had come about this cornucopia of passports honestly.

Development of the School's normal year-round business crept upwards at a painfully slow rate and so we were keen to maximise our summer income as much as possible. We had some new clients for our teenage summer school. One client, Marisa Balzarini, was to become a lifelong friend and the most loyal and long-lasting customer in the history of the School, and two clients were amongst the most short-lived business contacts.

We only ever had one group from Norway in all the years we operated the School. The group had been generated through the recommendation of a teacher on one of our 1981 teachers' courses who had recommended us to a colleague. There were nine fifteen and sixteen year olds, mainly girls. The latter were mature beyond their years. The group had a male and a female group leader, both were young and neither was capable of, or interested in, exercising any form of discipline. They took no part in the evening social activities, preferring to spend their evenings in pubs unencumbered by their students.

The first signs of trouble were not long in coming. The students had insisted on staying in pairs instead of allowing us to place them singly together with a student of another nationality. There

---

[1] *The favourite expression of one of our most faithful of travel agent clients, Mara Martinovitch, when in moments of adversity.*

were all kinds of trials and tribulations which I will not burden the reader with, but instead tell the tale of a pair of girls staying in Devizes Road.

We had a ten o'clock curfew and students were expected to be at home by that time. The two girls in question generally were. However, towards the end of the first week the host family discovered that the girls waited until the family had gone to bed and then "escaped" through their down stairs bedroom window and went off to town. They returned much later by the same route.

The family reported this to Barbro and we called in the group leaders to a meeting with the girls. They were told that this was a serious matter which we would not tolerate. The girls agreed that they would not do it again. The leaders were vaguely amused by the whole matter but gave some semblance of support.

Two days later the host family phoned to say that the girls had done their disappearing trick again two nights running and the desperate husband in the family had nailed the windows shut to prevent a further occurrence. That should have been the end of trouble with the girls, but more was to come.

One evening in the middle of the last week of their course, Barbro got a frantic phone call from the host family to say that they had a screaming female neighbour outside of their house trying to get hold of one of the Norwegian girls. The neighbour claimed that the girl had paid a visit to her house when she was out and had seduced her husband, a fact that the girl did not deny. The situation was getting ugly, there was nothing for it but to rescue the two girls from the vengeful wife and find another family in a different part of town, before the police were called. Barbro successfully extricated them and the next day we sought to return them to the land of their birth. With no support from the leaders this was impossible and for the next two days before their planned departure we feared each ring of the phone lest it might bring new bad tidings of the terrible two.

In July we appointed Elizabeth Keatinge, to work half time as my assistant. Elizabeth was one of our most loyal host "mothers" and she was a tremendous support. She presented us with further experience of armed service officer wives. We were already aware of the strong military presence to the north of Salisbury. Both she and a succession of EFL teacher army wives were really interesting, confident people who had travelled widely. In general they got on extremely well with students and were very popular. Unfortunately for us they seldom stayed long as they had to follow their husbands as they were moved around the world.

During the same summer we had our first Spanish speaking group from an agent called Tamara on the Canary Islands. We gave the agency an allocation of places, but when we received the list of students we found that they had grossly exceeded the number of places offered. Despite our entreaties to shorten the list, the agency insisted that they had already booked the tickets, the parents had paid and they would have all sorts of legal problems if we could not take the whole group. So, we found ourselves, inexperienced as we were, with a group of over fifty Canary Islanders.

As it turned out, Barbro was able to find enough accommodation and we enjoyed having the lively youngsters in the School, but for two things. The first difficulty we had was getting the children to come to school when it was raining. On the first occasion this happened we could not understand where all the students were at class start time. A few phone calls to host families revealed that the children would not leave the house in the rain. The group leader explained to us that the children never went to school at home in "bad" weather. This was a habit we soon broke.

The second novelty for us was rather more serious. I have mentioned that it was possible to enter the cellar to the School from the street. The cellar which I had refurbished, was available to students as a leisure facility and they frequently met there during break times. One afternoon I was checking the door to the cellar when I found blood on the ground. I hastened into the cellar to be greeted by the sight of what appeared to be a mystical ceremony. A circle of girls was seated around a table in the middle of which was a lighted candle. One girl was standing over another, doing something to her head. When the group saw me they scattered, all apart from the standing girl and the one sitting under her. I put on the lights and beheld a gruesome scene. The seated girl was bleeding from both ears, through one of which was a needle.

Our cellar had been turned into an ear piercing salon! There were tufts of bloodied cotton wool on the floor and several needles by the candle. The latter had been used to "sterilise" the needles. At a subsequent parade of students we ascertained that only a few ears had been pierced by the time I stopped the operation, nevertheless much blood had been spilt. Fortunately, none of those who had been operated on succumbed to blood poisoning.

At the end of August we ran our first training course for teachers going to work in Sweden. Nick McIver ran the course and not unexpectedly, was so successful that he ran all the subsequent courses at the specific request of the Swedish staff.

During the autumn our flow of one-to-one students steadily increased but we had, and were to continue for many years to have, great difficulty in getting profitable group class averages. Our positive summer cashflow was soon reversed to an outflow.

Once again as Christmas approached, we made plans to visit our Swedish family and again we were to finance the trip by selling and transporting a trailer load of books. Our journey took the same route as before, Harwich to Gothenburg by ferry and then a long drive to Uppsala. We had heard of threatened strikes by white collar workers in Sweden, but we did not think that this would affect us. However, on the boat there was much discussion amongst passengers about how the country was paralysed by the strikes. A couple of hours before the ferry docked a smartly dressed Swedish gentleman came up to me and said that he had heard our little daughters telling someone that they were going to Uppsala to see their Swedish grandparents. He introduced himself as a Swedish air force officer and told us that he had been intending to take a train to his home in Västerås, (which was on our route to Uppsala), but that the whole Swedish rail network was at a standstill. He offered us a meal at his house if we would give him a lift. I explained that I had very little space in the car and that there would be some delay as I had to get customs clearance for my cargo, (this time I had all the documentation and cash to pay the VAT). He was undeterred and we arranged to meet by the customs office after I had cleared my goods.

The ship came in at 16.00. It was already dark and the snow was falling as we drove off the ferry. I diverted from the queue of cars heading to the exit customs control, to the commercial clearance facility. I sat and waited in a queue of heavy goods vehicles, our way out being blocked by closed iron gates. After a considerable time in the queue, during which we had not seen a single customs officer checking the vehicles, our intending passenger knocked on my window which I opened, letting in the freezing air.

"They are on strike apart from one officer and he is preventing all commercial vehicles from leaving."

We were wedged in between lorries and vans and there was no way of extricating ourselves unless permitted to do so by their frustrated drivers.

"You may have to stay here all night until more staff come on duty tomorrow!" he announced before he dashed off through the snow in the direction of the office.

The thought of spending a freezing, hungry night in the car with three small children and an increasingly exasperated wife was not attractive.

Our ally from Västerås returned to the car.

"Have you got all the documents and the money ready for customs clearance?"

"Yes, here."

I showed him the papers and the cash.

"Give it to me."

I handed over the envelope and he disappeared in the direction of the office again. He soon reappeared with the customs policeman who took a quick look into our trailer. The official then moved over to a lorry which was blocking our way and told the driver to move forward enough for us to get out. He came over to me and shiftily said, "You realise that you will get no receipt for this money?"

The awful truth then dawned on me that the wily air force officer had bribed the policeman with my cash! Our passenger jumped in with his suitcase and said, "Get going while you have the chance."

The gate was held open for me by the policeman and we were on our way. I spent the next six hours driving with quick glances in the rear view mirror expecting to see flashing blue lights!

Chapter 6   Accommodation

For the whole period of operation of the School, Barbro was responsible for accommodation and Welfare. Little wonder therefore that at every British Council inspection, except one, this section of the report was always graded as a point of excellence.

While there were always challenges, Barbro had the patience and empathy to win over, mollify or console, intransigent, misunderstood and distressed students and group leaders. And there were plenty of them. Often, there were cultural or adjustment difficulties. Spoilt children who were used to having a maid to dress them, group leaders who insisted that their children did not need to return home in the evenings until midnight, adult students who were used to going everywhere by car now finding they had a twenty minute walk to school, and so on and so on. Sometimes we got the impression that some students got more love and attention at school than they got at home. A case of paedophilia in the student's home country came to light; children with difficult home backgrounds found some solace in the School and, tragically, cases of child alcoholism and mental disorder were identified through counselling. But in relation to the population of the School the proportion of this sometimes vociferous minority was indeed a very small, though time consuming.

However, Barbro's main preoccupation at all times was finding enough, and the right sort, of beds. Increasingly, through the years as the School grew, this meant a longer and longer working day. Quite early on in the School's history it was necessary to employ an assistant for Barbro, and with the exception of a couple of spectacular failures, Barbro found people to help her who were in tune with her high standards.

By 2004 we had around 350 host families on our register. Each of these had had to have an initial visit and then a biannual revisit. Even this number was not enough to satisfy summer demand and during the period from the beginning of May until the end of July Barbro's working day seldom finished before 2300. My working day, though long, allowed me to arrange supper each evening and take it to the School for Barbro and anyone else who was working late.

Sue Reeder, Barbro's last assistant

Despite the difficulties involved in finding enough families to house our burgeoning summer school population, Barbro's philosophy was that there is always a suitable bed to be found somewhere and she and her assistant always managed to find one.

Barbro was always keen to make the host families feel part of the school organisation. Each Christmas we had a host family get together with wine, coffee and mince pies. Some of the families were interested in having a look around the school and to meet the teachers they had heard about from their students. Each year we had an informal sweepstake among the staff to see which host family would eat the most mince pies. The odds were shortest on Mr and Mrs C. They always managed at least eight pies between them.

The rate of increase in size of the summer school brought with it requests for residential accommodation. Our first attempt at providing residential accommodation was at the Theological College in the Cathedral Close. The position was very attractive and the historic building was charming, but the standard of accommodation was somewhat basic. It seemed that priests in training embraced Spartan ideals. This ancient building was not really suited to occupation by boisterous teenagers and there were bound to be complaints from the staid occupants of the exclusive nearby properties.

However, my biggest challenge there was not the children but an adult, the Italian mother of one of the children, who had accompanied the group. This woman found her way into the College kitchen on the first day and started to advise the chefs about how to prepare food for her son. Her frequent visits to the kitchen eventually resulted her being chased out of the kitchen by a knife wielding chef. He insisted that either she went or he would leave. Fortunately, the group leader was a very sane person who assisted me when I expelled the mother from the College.

Our second attempt to provide residential accommodation in Salisbury anticipated the likelihood of Italian mothers deciding that English food was not for their children. We took over the White House guest house for a month and the groups staying there brought their own cook and a huge supply of pasta. However, this was not an ideal arrangement, there were no proper leisure facilities for the children and the rooms were not really suitable for our purpose with mainly double beds.

Unable to find alternative residential accommodation in Salisbury and excluded from nearby possibilities by the fact that other schools already had established occupancy, in 1994 we contracted with Bruton School, about an hour west of Salisbury, to rent accommodation.

Despite many early requests from clients to use this accommodation, enrolments were painfully slow and not until the beginning of June could we breathe a huge sigh of relief when we saw that we would be able to fulfil the contract requirements and avoid a substantial financial penalty. We used Bruton for two summers. In the second year Anna was appointed to manage the site. This centre was never really satisfactory, partly because of the distance from Salisbury (part of our market appeal was that we could offer residential, and homestay accommodation; some groups were split between the two centres), but mainly because teachers and group leaders were worried about the danger posed by the main road which ran through the School site.

I had always wanted to run courses on the Isle of Wight and in 1996 we had the good fortune to find a residential centre on the Isle of Wight, at Upper Chine School. Anna was manager there in summer 1996, Easter 1997 and summer 1997.

In 1995 we had a major stroke of luck when one of our main competitors in Salisbury, ILC, decided to pull out of the city and to close their centre. In the summer time, they had been using classrooms at the Godolphin School in Salisbury. Their departure meant that we could make a bid for these classrooms and two years later we started using their residential accommodation. Godolphin was just five minutes' walk from our centre at Fowlers Road, an ideal position for us. We could now offer residential accomodation and homestay accommodation to young learners and adult courses for groups of mixed ages.

In 1998, Anna took over the management of the Godolphin site and soon achieved legendary status among our clients because of her competence and boundless energy. She built a team of enthusiastic colleagues and managed the site for many years, gaining the respect of the very demanding Godolphin School Bursars. Soon we were using all of the facilities and even installing extra beds to increase the capacity in the summers. The expansion of the residential courses was phenomenal and soon we out-grew Godolphin.

Another stroke of luck came our way when Salisbury College, with whom we had an agreement to rent classrooms for homestay students, announced that they were building a residential facility for their degree course students. In 2002 we were the first occupants of the brand new building, St Mary's. However, and to our regret, another school in the town had inveigled their way into hiring a part of the building. This led to a number of difficulties relating to responsibility for student welfare and care. Fortunately for us, Anna's style of management was seen to be far superior to that of our competitor and they were not permitted use of the building the following year. We placed older teenagers on this site and from the second year occupied all 100 beds.

It would not be just to leave the subject of accommodation without relating some anecdotes, humorous and tragic.

In later years the mobile phone was a blessing to us in many ways, in particular at weekends when communicating with couriers. However, as it became more prevalent for children to have their own phones, difficulties arose. Students from South America and the Far East got calls from parents in the middle of the night, much to the annoyance of host families, boyfriends and girlfriends at home also called at unsociable hours. Hardly a day passed when some child had not lost a phone on a bus or in MacDonald's, but most troublesome was the tendency of students to phone parents about anything which bothered them instead of talking to their group leader.

A dramatic result of the latter trend occurred just before Christmas 2004. Two sixteen year-old Italian girls, part of a large group, were alone in the house, the host family having gone to some evening function. We received a phone call on the emergency phone from the Italian Embassy in London to say that two girls were being threatened by a chanting mob with lighted candles. They requested that we report this to the Salisbury police immediately. Our experience of getting a response from Salisbury police station was poor, so we set off to investigate. However, before we reached the address we received another phone call, this time from the host family. They had come home to find the girls terrified and barricaded in their room. What they had seen at the front door was a group of carol singers who had, in the normal way, knocked at the door after singing.

The girls, fearing for their lives, had phoned their parents. The parents in a blind panic had contacted the emergency number of the Italian Embassy in London and the charming tradition of carol singing had been transformed into an international terror incident.

On a few occasions, we had to take in errant students to our own home for a night. Generally, this was when youngsters had come by alcohol and were in no fit state to stay with a host family. However, the most traumatic such occurrence was quite different and really was very unpleasant for us. We had an agent in Panama who occasionally sent us long stay adult students. Students from Panama needed a visa and we had always successfully arranged this. One Sunday afternoon we received a phone call from what was then called "Immigration Control" at Heathrow airport to say that they had detained a twenty two year-old female who claimed that she was going to attend a course with us. This was quite correct and I confirmed it so. "We are refusing her entry to the United Kingdom," said the official.

I remonstrated with him but to no avail. "We require her to return to Panama by the earliest possible flight which is on Monday evening. In the meantime, you are responsible for her."

I asked what this entailed and was aghast to hear that the woman was to be taken to Salisbury in the taxi we had arranged and I had to act as her gaoler until she could take the flight home. She was literally expected to be under some form of custody with us until she was driven back to the airport.

The girl arrived at our home in a very distressed state. She had little English and we had had no time to find a Spanish speaker to help us. Not surprisingly, she was angry and confused and the next twenty four hours were exceedingly awkward for us. At home she chose to spend most of her time in her room but joined us for meals, hardly jolly occasions, until with great relief we were able to bundle her into a taxi on Monday afternoon.

No trouble was too great for Barbro in trying to meet the requests of clients when it came to accommodation arrangements. Thus it was when the male leader of an Austrian group of school children announced that he would be bringing a female teacher, his fiancée, with him and he would like to have double bed accommodation for the two of them, that Barbro identified a suitable host family with such a facility.

Now, this happened in the days before emails and faxes. For urgent correspondence we used the services of a local company with a telex. We delivered telexes to their office and they delivered replies to us or dictated them on the phone.

The Austrian group arrived quite late on a Friday evening. The distribution of students to host families took place and finally the two leaders were whisked away by their hosts.

Next morning, when we arrived at the School, there was an envelope on the front door mat. Barbro opened it and from my office I heard a howl. "Oh no….." The contents of the envelope were soon in my hand. It was a telex which read, "My fiancé too ill to travel. I have arranged for another female teacher to accompany the group, please arrange her single accommodation."

Barbro was distraught and sat in her office dreading the moment when the door opened and the leaders came in. This duly happened, the male leader came in and immediately the crestfallen accommodation supremo stared to gush apologies.

"Oh, it really doesn't matter, it was quite interesting in fact," said the Austrian. The female leader came in followed by some of the children and so the subject was dropped.

Four years later, we had Austrian visitors; it was the two group leaders who Barbro had inadvertently bedded together, now married, with their two children.

Chapter 7   Finance

Clients best forgotten

I cannot think of another field in the world of commerce where a supplier is so trusting of the customer, or generally the customer's agent, as that of the EFL industry. Often we gave substantial credit to people we had never met and for whom it was impossible to get trade references. In the last few years, schools have co-operated much more closely with each other to warn of bad risks or even to supply credit references, but this is a fairly recent development.

Yet it is a remarkable fact that with a few notable exceptions, we always got paid. I would estimate that over the period of our ownership of the School we had a turnover of over £30 million, yet our bad debts over that time amounted to less than £30,000. Nevertheless, losing any money hurt us, especially in the early years when our financial situation was at its most parlous. But it was also extremely irksome to find that a very few people of purported high ethical standards just pocketed the money and cheated us.

Caracas,. 16 August 2004

Dear Mitchell*,

Greetings and God Bless,

I am again on Caracas, I just arrived yesterday night.
Could you please send me ASAP the total amount we own you as we will pay it as soon we receive it, excuse me but it was not possible to make the wire on Miami due the climatic (hurricane) problems.

Last week my son send you an e-mail asking this charge to my credit card, as the father at the children had call me early today because they do no not has pocket money, could you please give them as soon you can today?.

$USD 490 ....and give it to SEABASTIAN, SARDO

$USD 500................and give it to JONATTAN, REYES

My Credit Card is;

Could you please indicate when it had been charged?.

Yours sincerely,

Oscar Mendoza

God bless the Salisbury School of English

*Janet Mitchell was our wonderful, long suffering, Accounts Manager.

Janet Mitchell

We had actually got a reference on this client before starting to work with him. But each year his excuses for delaying payment got more outlandish. Faulty credit cards, currency restrictions, floods and hurricanes were usually blamed and part payments of accounts in dollars led to the most horrendous calculations for Janet. His specialty was to try to carry a debt forward against the promise of more business. The last straw was when a cheque for $8000 sent to us with what seemed quite apposite, a picture of him praying, bounced. We decided that enough was enough.

The situation a school can get into when a group organiser does not pay is frustrating in the extreme. We once had a group sent to us by a school in Paris, Ecole Musique. It was a residential course and we had to arrange for music practice facilities for the children. We had received the 10% deposit in good time and had no reason not to expect the rest of the money to arrive prior to the course. It did not. Despite calls to the course organiser who was to accompany the group we could not get any response to our requests for payment.

We had no option but to arrange the transfer for the children to get to Salisbury and to welcome them in the normal way, after all they had probably all paid the school and it was through no fault of theirs that the school had not paid us. I met with the course organiser and he coolly announced to me that the school would pay us at the end of the course if they were satisfied with our services. What could I do? If I refused to honour any part of our course arrangements the children would suffer and like as not, we would not get paid. No, we had to treat the group like any other and do our best for them.

I have heard of some schools trying extreme measures such as refusing to return the students' passports until money appeared. This is probably illegal, but I can understand their desperation.

The Ecole Musique returned to France at the end of their successful course which had been enhanced for them by the use of expensively hired musical instruments and did not pay us another penny. The sum involved justified us using an international debt collection agency, but it was to no avail. Exactly the same ruse was used the same year by a Thai agent, this the one and only Thai group we ever had.

So our bad debt league table was in order of value, Venezuela, France, Thailand and.......England! On two occasions we fell afoul of superficially respectable English gentlemen who knocked on our door offering students. In one case a retired Air Force Officer with strong connections in the Middle East supplied us with a string of Gulf Air Force cadets who were destined to do pilot training in the UK. They were excellent students and we were very happy with the arrangement until our English contact defaulted on several successive payments. His partner, whom we did not know, had absconded with our money.

The second case was where a local man, R. G., simply refused to pay the £2000 he owed us for a course we had arranged for some of his clients. With the wisdom of hindsight I should have taken him to the small claims court. When I last heard of him he was standing for Parliament.

Another English debt which caused us much anxiety was with the military attachés' office in London of a Middle Eastern country. We had had a number of military personnel from this office and they had run up a debt of over eighteen thousand pounds. I was desperate to recover this money, but my faxes and phone calls were not responded to.

I travelled to London and found the office. Not surprisingly, there was strict security around the building and surveillance cameras. I tried to gain entry but was told that I had to have an appointment. I watched the entrance for a while and noted that the only visitors permitted entrance were Arabs. They went to the door and announced themselves on an intercom on the door post. I waited for my chance and when I saw an Arab gentleman approach the door I walked right up behind him. As he walked through the door I pushed in behind him.

The clerks in the office were quite alarmed to see me and wondered how I had got in. I announced my business and waved copies of the invoices. A senior clerk was summoned and I explained my mission. I was asked to sit and wait. Twenty minutes later I was called to the counter and presented with a cheque for the full amount! I rushed off to the nearest branch of Lloyds and banked the cheque just in case they thought to cancel it after my departure.

By far the greatest proportion of our income came from Italy, Spain and Japan and although we had some slow payers we always got our money in the end. However, one transaction in Italy almost bankrupted us.

The School's greatest financial problem through the first half of its existence was under-capitalisation. We never had enough capital to feel secure that we could survive the next winter, to invest in promotion or to upgrade furniture and equipment. I could not even afford to pay myself a salary until 1985, surviving on my savings alone. So I was constantly on the lookout for any income streams which might bolster our finances. I was very interested therefore when in 1984 the Secretary of a property company, Nova Holdings, our landlords, came to see me with a business proposal. He, Mr Oglethorpe, was a lawyer and though he seemed to take life very seriously indeed he was a pleasant and honourable man to deal with.

Mr Oglethorpe explained that one of his clients, P. N., was a local woman who had married an Italian and lived in Turin. He had represented her family's affairs for many years and knew her well. According to him she ran a successful language school there. However, she was looking for a way in which she could reduce the costs of the British teachers she employed. Apparently, the teachers' salaries were subject to an employer's tax of 40%. He asked if I would be prepared to employ her teachers and "lend" them to Mrs N. This way the teachers would have the advantage of their National Health and pension rights being safeguarded in the UK and the employer would be paying around 10% of their salaries as contributions. I could charge 10% of the salaries for the service and Mrs N. would still save 20%.

Now, I am aware that today this would be quite illegal, but then it was not and indeed a senior partner in a law firm had proposed it to me. I first checked the viability of the scheme with my accountants and then went ahead. I drew up the teacher contracts and soon I had five more employees, who I had never met. The scheme should have netted me around six thousand pounds a year.

All went well for the first two months. I opened an Italian bank account to pay the teachers and Mrs N. sent me the agreed monthly payment. And then the payments stopped. My client claimed that things were not going too well for the School just then, but that she was expecting a major customer to place a large order with them. However, in the meantime would I be prepared to do a consultancy job to look at the School's finances and to prepare a business plan? I saw that this was very much in my interests and agreed a fee with her for doing so.

I duly flew to Turin for three days. I was given an office space and access to all the company records which were of course in Italian. The texts were difficult for me to understand but the figures were not. The School was in a precarious situation. The fact that I had five employees working there, each on a contract with three months notice gave me the ghastly realisation that if the School went down, mine could too. Clearly, Mr Oglethorpe had been duped by his client and he had inadvertently landed me in a heap of trouble.

I prepared a list of recommendations for the School that included spending cuts, but I also identified the most profitable parts of the business and suggested that she should concentrate on these. On the last evening I decided to treat myself to a decent meal. I had been staying in a hotel near to the station and I wandered around and found what appeared to be a good restaurant. My judgement must have been impaired by the desperation I was feeling.

I walked in through the lobby of the restaurant at the end of which was a low desk with a girl sitting behind it. On her desk was a pile of what looked like passports. I asked if she spoke English.

"Yes, what do you want?" I told her I wanted a table. "You just want to eat?"

"Yes, of course."

She called out to another woman who led me through a large set of double doors. The doors were open and in their place was a heavy curtain that we pushed through. Inside there was a huge room filled with white table-clothed tables. I chose a place by the opposite wall so that I could sit with my back to the wall and observe the comings and goings in the restaurant. And there were plenty.

My order was taken and I sat back to think about the last three days over a glass of red wine. The first thing I noticed was that all the diners were men. I had the naive thought that perhaps this was a gentlemen's club. Then I saw that every now and again the woman who had shown me to my table would come in, march up to a table and soon after, the diner would leave and go through the curtained doors. Neither was it one way traffic. Just as often men would come in, one at a time and walk to a table and sit down.

A movement on the floor distracted my fascination with this activity. I looked down and immediately recognised a parade of cockroaches marching across the floor away from the wall. Inspection of the wall behind me showed that reinforcements were crawling out of holes in the wallpaper. I pushed my table forward carefully so as not to upset my wine carafe but to give a decent margin of distance between the creatures and me. I suppose that I should have left then, but it was all too interesting and what happened next added to the bizarre nature of my experience. The curtains parted and two children, around twelve years of age, a boy and girl dressed very smartly each with a document under their arms, bowed in the entrance. There was a ripple of applause from the diners. The girl turned right, the boy left. Each in their own direction they strode to a waiting piano at both ends of the room. They both then opened their respective piano lids, sat down, put the music which they had carried with them on to the music stands and turned their heads to look at each other, and nodded. The sound of the cockroach march was drowned out by the cacophony of two young pianists playing a duet with pianos so far away from each other that the time lag caused by the distance between them made their timing impossible. Fortunately it only lasted about fifteen minutes during which time I was distracted by the arrival of my food.

I don't remember how long it was before it dawned on me that I was dining in one huge cockroach infested brothel.

Once back in England I went to see Mr Oglethorpe and told him that he had landed me in a very risky situation that could lead to a substantial bad debt. We agreed that I should give the teachers two months notice and break off dealings with Mrs N. However, although he administered a substantial estate on behalf of her family he could not arrange repayment of the debt in a lump sum. He proposed that the allowance, which he paid to Mrs N. from a family trust, should be diverted to pay the debt to the school off in instalments. I had no choice but to accept. Our working capital was thus denuded until, four years later the full amount had been paid.

Property and premises

Jane Rycroft
(later Lewis)

In 1987, at the height of the property boom, we decided that since we were operating out of a leasehold building, it would be good for the company to buy a small house as an investment, which could be sold later at a profit to provide a deposit for a freehold site for the School. Property prices were like that then, they just rose and rose. We had no problem in getting a £40,000 mortgage for a three bed-roomed house in Kelsey Road. We spent some time and money on refurbishing the property and then let it. Our first tenant was in fact an employee, Jane Rycroft, a lady of considerable talent and determination who developed her career from that of our secretary when she was first employed by the School in May 1988, to RSA diploma qualified teacher.

This arrangement was very satisfactory from our point of view until the time came to move the School in 1989. Then things happened so quickly that we did not have time to sell the property in Kelsey Road.

In October 1987 an entrepreneurial estate agent sent me the sales prospectus of a property in Fowlers Road. The building was a Montessori school. The owner, Miss Nesta Brinn, was considering downsizing her operation. Thus the building was for sale. The asking price was £230,000, far beyond our reach. The situation of this School and the size, were ideal for us and we spent several tortuous months anguishing over various ways of financing a purchase, including selling our home. In the event, the building was withdrawn from sale in April 1988 as Miss Brinn could not get planning permission for change of use on the smaller building she wished to move to.

Our lease at 14 Rollestone Street had upward only rent reviews every three years and the next review was due in 1989. From our experience of the previous reviews we expected a further substantial increase. Our deliberations concerning Fowlers Road had unsettled us to the extent that we had decided that we had to raise the profitability of the School in order to save capital for an eventual freehold purchase.

It was self evident that 14 Rollestone Street was far too big for our operation for ten months of the year. It was equally obvious that our rent was soon to increase further. We decided to shed the yoke of the onerous lease and to move to smaller premises. We would make more use of temporary, hired premises in the summer time for our growing seasonal business. We agreed with the landlords that we could advertise the leasehold for sale and to our great surprise, a local firm of stockbrokers offered us a premium of £25,000.

We found a small suite of offices in Chipper Lane in central Salisbury and agreed a rent with the landlord. He agreed to allow us to rebuild the premises to our specification, as three classrooms and an office.

On 31st October 1988 we handed the keys of Rollestone Street to the stockbrokers and moved our goods the short distance to Chipper Lane. As I was carrying boxes up the stairs to our new second floor premises I was called to the phone. It was the estate agent who had tried to sell us the

Montessori school premises. He told me that the property was once more on the market as Miss Brinn had got her planning permission on appeal.

Now we were thrown into a new dilemma! We had made a substantial financial commitment to the new premises and had signed a 15 year lease. Yet, we really wanted the Fowlers Road school. I contacted my accountant, Peter Smith, to discuss the situation with him. He asked me to tidy up my business plan so that we could discuss it together and arranged to come from Haslemere to see me on 14th November.

Our meeting duly took place and then he said, "Let's go to Lloyds Bank." We had no appointment but Peter told the person at the information desk that he wished to see the manager. He took my business plan and the estate agent's prospectus and told me to wait for him in the foyer. Fifteen minutes later he came out.

"Right, I've got you £230,000 at 15% variable interest."

The fact that the interest rate was so horrendous did not dampen my joy. In fact this was fairly typical at the time. (In February 1990, even my home mortgage with Abbey National was at 15.4% interest).

I went back to my office and made an offer to the estate agent of £220,000 for 36 Fowlers Road, subject to survey. This was accepted. I set the whole purchase in train with my bewildered solicitors who had only just completed on Chipper Lane.

In fact the surveyors report was quite worrying. There were a number of issues to be dealt with the most urgent of which was that the roof was collapsing. The previous owner had changed the light slate roof for heavy concrete tiles. Fortunately, one of my Rotarian friends was a structural engineer and he designed an extensive steel cage to reinforce the roof. This and other improvements we wished to make were priced at £20,000 by our builders. I tried to get the price of the building reduced by this amount but in the end compromised at £210,000. We just had enough cash through the loan to buy the building and do the repairs.

As ever, things did not quite work out as neatly. As the work progressed we identified more items for improvement and we sank all our available capital into the project.

I had taken a huge gamble; I now had the challenge of getting rid of Chipper lane, and in a hurry. We could not afford a mortgage at 15% and the rent of our leasehold. I put Chipper Lane on the market while we were still hanging curtains and pictures there!

While all this was going on we had to keep a semblance of order and continuity for our current students and for visiting agents. We had suddenly become very busy at Chipper Lane, we had won a contract with the Angolan government to take a group of ten coastguards over nine months to bring their English up to a level where they could move to Norway to receive training on fishery protection vessels.

On Friday 16th December 1988, the last day of school for the year, we received a visit from a Mr Trythall and a friend. Mr Trythall had been running EFL classes at his home. They were interested in taking over our lease at Chipper Lane for their embryonic language school.
 Later, they made an offer of a premium of £15,000. This just about covered the amount we had spent on the building. I was faced with a dilemma. I badly needed to unload this leasehold, but by selling to Mr Trythall I would be letting a competitor into the City.

I decided to sell, and on 31st of January 1989 we moved out of Chipper lane and into Fowlers Road. A decision I was never to regret. In fact, we got some benefit from selling to Mr Trythall. Not infrequently some of his students would transfer to us.

When we had finished the repairs to 36 Fowlers Road we had depleted our cash reserves and spent the entire bank loan. Yet, we still had a building in a poor state of decoration and the garden was really quite unsuitable for students to use as it was on a steep slope. In 1989 and into 1990 we spent every available penny on upgrading the building. Some decorating we did ourselves, some was done by a local firm, the cheapest we could find.

I hired a mechanical excavator and practised the skills I had learnt on our small holding in Sweden. I levelled the garden and then with Mr Burke the gardener's help landscaped the lawns and made a terrace. Gradually, the state of the premises approached the standard we aspired to. But money was always in short supply and in December 1989 we were forced to put the property in Kelsey Road on to the market. By this time, with high interest rates, it was difficult to sell and we had to spend money on improving the roof and the drains. I noted in my personal diary on 30th January, "I look forward with trepidation to completing on Kelsey Road. It would be an enormous financial and psychological relief." On 9th February 1990 I got a call from my solicitor to say that the house deal had been completed at £65,000. This gave us a welcome profit, less the expenses we had incurred in the refurbishment of the house, to spend on Fowlers Road.

This was a very difficult time for us as in the beginning of February 1990 Swedish banks were on strike and since much of our business was coming from Sweden, we were receiving no payments.

At that time the weather was against us too with heavy rains which found leaks in the conservatory at Fowlers Road and at home. In fact the stormy weather nearly cost me my life. On 25th January, as President of Salisbury Chamber of Commerce and Industry, I had to attend a meeting of the Confederation of Chambers of Commerce in Southampton. This was the day of the famous "hurricane". The entry in my diary says, "I arrived late because of blocked roads. As I got out of the car after parking, I narrowly escaped death when steel roof sheeting from the Post House Hotel, sailed over my car and crashed to the ground beside me. Later all roads to Salisbury were blocked so I took a route through the New Forest, frequently diverting because of fallen trees. Quite hair-raising! Five overturned lorries on Pepperbox hill. At home there were 8 tiles off our roof and there was damage to the School building, the side wall to the back entrance of the School had collapsed."

Internationella Skolorna (IS)

Our Swedish agent, IS, was a branch of the educational trust which I had worked for in Sweden. The trust owned schools in Aix en Provence, teaching French, and Munich, teaching German. The managing director of the trust, Anders Höglund was a very respected and old friend of mine, so when he approached me in September 1990 with a proposal to buy 51% of our school, I listened.

His proposal was that the Salisbury School of English should become part of the IS group and benefit from the group's combined marketing and other resources. Barbro and I would retain our positions and we would also retain the building. He offered £50,000 for the 51% share. At the time this offer was flattering, we had only occasionally made a yearly profit, and more often we had made a loss.

Barbro and I considered this proposal long and hard.

The thought of financial stability and investment in the marketing of the School was very attractive.
We had had a very tough year. In February storms had exposed some weaknesses in the fabric of the building. I had done a lot of work with a local builder to repair leaks and water damage, things which our insurance would not pay out for. Money spent on this meant that we had no funds for landscaping the garden and so I spent many hours in the evenings and at weekends through the summer doing block work and concreting. All through the autumn of 1990 I had spent my weekday evenings and weekends insulating, flooring and putting up partitions in the attic. Barbro and I realised that in the long run this degree of personal manual labour was unsustainable; I had to concentrate on the administration and promotion of the School.

From left to right, MW, Anna Clara Sainte Rose, (IS Aix-en-Provence), Anders Hoglund, Britt Werneberg, (IS Stockholm), Gerhard Bruchner, (IS Munich).

The School was also suffering badly from the effects of the first Gulf War which had started in August 1990, our student numbers had declined as international travel diminished and our financial prospects looked grim. At times cash flow was dire. I had a £30,000 overdraft facility at a punitive rate of interest, which I was often forced to use. Shortage of cash sometimes got so bad that I had to make a decision about who to pay, staff, host families or the VAT bill. My priority was always the former two, though often Barbro and I postponed our own salary payments, and by some miracle I was never late with the VAT.

We were worried about losing our independence, but I knew that I could work with and trust Anders. In addition, the Principals of the French and German schools were very old friends of ours and we knew that we would get on well. We decided to accept the offer on condition that all legal and accounting costs were paid by the buyer. The sale took place at the beginning of 1991.

Thus began an intensive period of rebranding the School and planning our joint promotion with the other two schools. Our meetings were constructive and often fun, and it was a bonus being able to spend time in Aix and Munich as well as Stockholm. We drew up a marketing plan for the first year which had us joint marketing at exhibitions in Moscow, Kiev and Berlin. Not only was our promotion subsidised but we got grants to equip our student computer suite, and some staff were assisted financially to take the RSA Diploma.

Things went well for the first three years. Our school grew and as we needed more space for classrooms and a new student common room, Barbro and I invested the payment we had received for the shares in a major extension of the School building. Then the blow fell! Anders, who was always extremely busy with his different areas of responsibility in Sweden, was instructed by his Board to delegate the management of IS to a new appointee.

A well meaning artist's impression of the IS Group's managers in the photo on page 52!

M. S. was duly appointed in Sweden. He had no experience of running a business and had previously been a scientist. But we had no choice, he was now our boss. We attended our first group meetings with him in the chair, with an open mind, but it was not long before messages started winging their way between the three Principals and the manager of the IS office in Stockholm expressing concern about M. S. management style. For the next four years we put up with this man but we were becoming increasingly disenchanted about membership of the IS group. I could say much about our concerns, but suffice it to say, that the man was totally unsuited to being a manager.

Fowlers Road with the new extension

We became so unhappy about the situation that I contacted Anders and said that we no longer wished to work with M.S. This was no news to Anders as the other two principals had his ear too.

We gave an ultimatum, either M.S goes or we do. This was bluff of the highest order as we had no other chance of employment. However, Anders had another solution. He suggested that we could buy back the 51% stake in the School which IS owned. That was a very typically friendly gesture. The downside was that M.S. was given the job of valuing the IS share of the business. He came up with a figure of £100,000 and we would have to pay our own legal expenses.

All of our cash had been sunk into the rebuilding of the School at Fowlers Road so Barbro and I were faced with the dilemma of how to finance the share purchase. Obviously the building had risen in value because of all the work we had done so I renegotiated the mortgage on the property to get some more cash. The terms of the new mortgage were that it should be fixed for ten years at 8.5%. This proved to be unnecessarily expensive for us over the next ten years as interest rates dropped, but we had little alternative. The remainder of the money was raised by remortgaging our home to the hilt.

In 1998 the School was once more our own!

Chapter 8   Foreign faces, foreign places

Reflections

In the hurly burly of professional life, the opportunity to take a pause and reflect seldom exists. Such mental capacity as one has tends to be fully engaged in the complicated process of making a living for one's family and employees through improving the prospects and performance of the company. It only occurred to me late in my career, that I and most of my colleagues, are incredibly privileged. The financial rewards of the EFL profession are not great but the opportunity to meet and touch the lives of hundreds, if not thousands of people from all over the world is almost unique. And, for those engaged in promoting their schools, the chance to travel and see parts of this planet which otherwise would just be a name to them, or indeed in many cases stay in places that they otherwise would never have heard of, is something very special. Yes, at times the inconvenience of travel, surly officials, long waits at airports, and occasionally the danger of actual harm, can dull the charm of the travel experience, but all in all, we were very lucky.

The privilege goes beyond just seeing the sights in far-flung places. The opportunity to get to know people in their own environments and gain some, though albeit perfunctory, insight into and understanding of their way of life, is a greatly enriching experience.

It is easy to view those you sell to, and in particular agents representing overseas buyers, as business associates only. I am ashamed to say that it was only late on in my career that I gained the realisation that most of these people had actually become my friends, that the development of trust, the endurance of setbacks and the sharing of success had paved the way for lasting and close friendships. In some cases this was equally true of students whose generosity in entertaining me, and in some cases, the whole of my family, in their own countries, was truly overwhelming.

In the pages that follow I write about some of my travels and experiences and tell a few tales about memorable people from different countries who have spent time with us. Of course this is only a sample and I implore the reader whose country has been excluded not to feel hurt, the length of this book has limits!

But first a word about "foreignness". We are all foreign somewhere, but the British often travel with an undeserved feeling that everyone else is foreign and they never are. Perhaps this is because we have the great good fortune to have a language that is totally dominant in world affairs. The worst manifestation of this effect, is a feeling of superiority over other peoples and a feeling that someone who does not speak English speaks an inferior language and thus must be inferior. I sometimes quote the story of a recent American President who, when resisting a bill to introduce compulsory Spanish lessons into schools is reported to have said "If English was good enough for Jesus Christ it is good enough for the American people".

My advice to all travellers to and from foreign parts, is to maintain your own moral and ethical standards, but to leave the cultural yardstick by which you judge others, at your airport of departure. People living in other countries and companies operating there should be judged by the standards of their own country. People's appearance, manners and behaviour are shaped by their own culture not by our own. When as travellers we react to the Italian art of queue jumping, the Chinese style of driving, the Japanese extreme formality or the risk of a stampede of people through a door which you hold open for a lady in Sweden, we must remember that this is their way, like it or loath it, abroad is different.

Czechoslovakia (Now the Czech Republic)

In 1989 we were all bemused by the rapidity of the decline of the Soviet Union, the fall of the Berlin Wall and the subsequent independence of East European states. All of us in the profession not only rejoiced that the Cold War was over, but that there was a huge new potential EFL market. My first visit to a country which had previously been part of the Soviet Union was to Prague in 1992. This had to be the most ill-conceived journey I have undertaken. We had been offered the opportunity of renting a flat in Prague, by an Italian friend. There was a language fair taking place on 31st January 1992 which I wanted to attend to appraise the potential of the Czech market. However, attending this would have meant that I would miss my daughter Sarah's eighteenth birthday, so I proposed that we should take her and Emma with us, (Anna was studying at university) and stay in the flat for a weekend. We could not afford to fly so I decided to drive to Prague.

We left for Dover on the morning of Tuesday 28th January. The first night we stayed in Belgium and the next day we drove all the rest of the way to Prague, a considerable distance. I had overlooked completely that there might be snow on the roads and incredibly, for the time of year, there was not. We found the flat; it was in a gloomy communist era building, and met the landlord. With an air of triumph he presented us with a tablet of soap and a toilet roll then disappeared. Later we understood why his gifts to us were so carefully proffered. When we went to the local so called supermarket, the shelves were almost devoid of goods. We saw that there were severe shortages of food and household items. It was a salutary experience for us and we had a terrible sense of guilt being able to use hard currency to get what we considered the necessities of life.

In the event, Sarah had an eye infection and spent most of the time in the flat. The rest of us explored the city. We experienced a strange mixture of feelings, there was exuberance among the people that the Russians had left, but the City had a tired and run down feel. It was extremely difficult to find a restaurant and when we did, there was no question of choosing from a menu, we had the only meal that was on offer.

We were able to visit the main sights before embarking on our return journey. The snow started as we left the City and we seemed to be just keeping ahead of it through Germany. There we discovered late on Sunday evening that German petrol stations did not accept credit cards. So we had to find a guest house with enough space for us and stay the night so that we could go to the bank the next day. We got back to Salisbury safely, but it had been a hare-brained scheme. However, we had had the unique opportunity of visiting Czechoslovakia before it became the Czech Republic in 1993 and seeing the recently liberated Prague before it became modern commercialised tourist venue.

Estonia

My second visit to an ex-Soviet Union country was to Estonia in 1993. This was two years after independence in September 1991, although there were still Russian troops in the country when I went there. My old employer, the Swedish Folkuniversitetet, had long had a partnership with the University of Tartu, a university founded by, and modelled on, Uppsala University. I managed to get a contact through the Swedish organisation, with an adult English teaching organisation which was part of Tartu University. I arranged to meet the manager and in May 1993, I paid my first visit to the country.

I was warmly received and it immediately became obvious that though there were many business opportunities, there was little money to fund them. Although the teaching facilities were reasonable there were no funds for modern teaching materials. One of the rooms in the School was the "copying room". A fulltime operative was copying UK text books for use in the classes. There were piles and piles of pirated pages spewing out of a copier which appeared to be in constant use. It was clear that it would be a time before much business for publishers or EFL schools came out of the country. However, I also realised that aid and investment were likely to flood into the country and that eventually there would be a market. It was a place to be in for the long haul.

There was huge interest in studying abroad, travel previously having been restricted to the Soviet Union, but again, little money to realise such hopes. Nevertheless I decided to persevere. The Head of the adult teaching organisation wanted to employ native English speakers for his classes. He knew that I was involved in recruiting teachers for Sweden and asked me to do the same for him. The stumbling block was of course the level of salary he could afford. Somehow he accessed enough funding for me to have a realistic chance of getting at least one teacher for him.

Tallinn TV Tower

In addition, he was interested in our courses for children. Estonian TV was showing a BBC English learning series called Muzzy in Gondoland. One of the co-authors of the series was a remarkably talented teacher working at SSE called Wendy Harris. Aware of the connection and a possible tie-in for SSE promotion, he set up a meeting for me with the head of children's educational programmes on Estonian television, to discuss the possibility of running an English quiz programme which would culminate in a televised final. The deal was that all the programmes would in some way relate to Salisbury and the prize would be a scholarship at the School for the winner.

I recall my meeting with the lady representing Estonian TV. We met for lunch in a restaurant at the top of the Television Tower in Tallinn. I was told that the tower, which is 312 metres high, was built by the Russians in 1980 to transmit television pictures of the Moscow Summer Olympics Sailing Regatta. Around the base of the tower there were bullet holes left from the attempted coup in 1991.

I have a poor head for heights and my appetite was much diminished when she insisted that we have a window seat. Trying to avoid looking at the view below the sheer overhang to the ground, my terror was compounded when the restaurant started rotating. I prayed that the Soviet concrete would survive long enough for me to get back to ground level. (Apparently the tower is now closed to visitors.) I do not remember too much about the meeting apart from the fact that we agreed the deal previously mentioned.

Subsequently, the TV series did take place for two years and I had the honour each year of going to Tallinn to present the prize. It was a wonderful occasion with hordes of incredibly enthusiastic children, and their ambitious parents, forming the audience to see the televised presentation. It was in fact a very moving and humbling experience. However, my hopes that the beneficence of the

Salisbury School of English would help some previously deprived Estonian child were dashed when the winner of the scholarship each year appeared to be very well connected to rich and powerful circles in Estonian society. Indeed the winner in the second year had been to England twice before, marking her family out to be well connected in the Soviet political circles.

The TV series did give us excellent publicity and a few paying students over the years. Unfortunately, the teacher recruitment scheme did not succeed as well. In the first term of the second year of the scheme, the male teacher from the UK, whom I had recently recruited, phoned me to say that he wanted to leave. I brought forward a visit to Tartu to see him. It transpired that while he was happy with the teaching situation and the town, he suspected that his flat was being used when he was not there. He said that sometimes when he returned from his classes the bedclothes had been moved and there was a distinct smell of smoke and sometimes perfume.

In the Tallinn TV studio

The flat had been provided by the School. It was well situated near the market square and the price was very reasonable. I found his claim bizarre but agreed to observe the flat for a while when he was having his afternoon classes. I felt extremely vulnerable and obvious hanging around the market square reading a newspaper in the snow. But sure enough, after a while a light came on in the flat and the blind was drawn. I considered all sorts of conspiracy theories but when I later recognised an official of the School coming out of the ground floor entrance to the flat together with a very attractive young woman, I drew the obvious conclusion. The teacher was not the only person with a key to the flat and the other keyholder knew exactly when the flat was going to be empty because he had access to the teacher's timetable.

My protest about this issue to the School, was met with a very frosty denial about anyone using the flat for post prandial liaisons. So frosty was the response that I suspected that I had only seen one of several who might be using the place. It was a sad end to a promising relationship with the School and I was left with the cost of repatriating the teacher.

Russia

Out of the blue, in late autumn 1993, I received an invitation to visit a potential agent in Moscow. While this might not seem remarkable now, it certainly was then. At that time it was quite exceptional to have Russian students or indeed contacts in Russia at all. After some correspondence it became clear that the lady who had contacted me, Livia, had recently formed a company and wished to send students to the UK. I was eager to meet her and thus arranged a visa and a flight to Moscow. She recommended the Hotel Ukraine and booked a room there for me. It was a huge

The Hotel Ukraine

60

building, with a tower in the middle and buildings on each side. I arrived at two o'clock on a Friday afternoon after an uneventful journey, apart from my first brush with the Ghengis Khan-like horde of taxi drivers aggressively toting for business at the Arrivals gate at the airport. The enormous foyer of the hotel was like a daylight disco with rock music blaring and girls, minimally dressed, draping languorously over the chairs in the reception area. They were attended by swarthy minders who were clearly not to be messed with.

I had not been in my room long before the phone started ringing and I was assailed with lubricious offers. I had to go on answering the phone as I was expecting a call from Livia. Eventually, she called. She asked me to wait outside the hotel by the main road, where she would pick me up at three thirty.

Well before the appointed time I was outside the hotel braving the bracing chill in the gathering gloom of a November afternoon. I soon became aware that I was very, very obvious and vulnerable. I was sharing a pick-up pitch with several ladies who were obviously not there for the fresh air. After rejecting a number of offers I decided to move away from the kerb as I was clearly bad for their business.

After what seemed to be an embarrassing eternity, a small car stopped near me. Since it did not excite the attention of my companions I realised that a woman was driving it. I walked over to the car and a woman in her thirties called out "Michael?" I confirmed my identity and went round to the passenger door. There ensued a fast and furious tour of nondescript backstreets while Livia explained that she was going to take me to her office where her colleagues were waiting, but she needed to ensure that she was not being followed. After a while we turned a bend and I recognised the unedifying edifice of the Hotel Ukraine. But before we reached the hotel, Livia turned into a side street and parked by a huge, monumental building which I had seen during my sojourn with

the ladies of the night. We left the car and she directed me towards this colossal building. We walked up the long series of steps, passing several armed guards in military uniform before entering through massive glass doors. Inside, a formidable posse of uniformed guards demanded Livia's ID and mine! I know not how, but I can guess, she got clearance for me and in we went. Before us was huge grim cavern of an entrance hall with a large staircase. Men and women, many in uniform, dashed to and fro, some greeting Livia and eying me suspiciously. "What is this place?" I asked Livia nervously. "This is the Ministry of Foreign Affairs of the Soviet Union," she replied. I was well aware of the fragility of the Soviet Union after the coup against Gorbachev and Yeltsin's election to President in June 1991. There certainly seemed to be a fairly feverish level of activity in the building.

The Ministry of Foreign Affairs

Needless to say I immediately suspected that I had been duped into some intrigue. I wondered how I could get out, but there was no point in trying, the place was swarming with uniforms. I thought that if they are going to interrogate me they are going to be awfully disappointed. And yet despite my horror at the position I was in, I noticed many odd details about my surroundings.

In this, the centre of Soviet power, on every landing there was a cigarette machine, not selling Russian cigarettes, but "Welcome to the Big Country – smoke Marlborough" was proclaimed in large neon signs.

I lamely followed Livia up several staircases to the third floor. She showed ID to a guard and we were admitted to a very large open plan office with heavy dark wooden furniture where a lot of people were busy typing and variously employed in office jobs. The sound of typing stopped as many heads looked up to survey the arrivals, me in particular. Several people left their desks and came to introduce themselves to me in perfect English. I have no idea what their normal day jobs were but they started firing questions at me about EFL course books, exams, the availability of teachers and so on. Eventually I was able to get a question in myself. I had realised that I was in no immediate danger, that I had celebrity status for some reason and that they must have a school here somewhere, but where was it? "Here" they said. Thoughts of becoming the sole English language provider to the Soviet Ministry of Foreign Affairs flashed through my mind in unison with a vision of piles of rouble notes.

After the frenzy of questions had subsided I was able to ascertain that the so called "school" was in the same building. Further, I was told that I could see it in action tomorrow. This seemed odd to me as the next day was Saturday. Livia led me off down the stairs and we went back to her car. Once more she drove me frantically round the backstreets, all the while looking in her back mirror. We stopped outside a dowdy looking restaurant, parked and she led me into a very Spartan room with plastic tables and chairs. The clientele looked sullen and threatening. Their morose attitudes were stirred when they heard Livia speaking English to me and I was eyed with a mixture of disdain and suspicion. Having ordered what I was guided to, Livia came to the point. "I am a Jehovah's Witness, are you?" Now, for the sake of business one may exaggerate some things, but even the avid, hungry for business salesman reaches a point where he realises that bluff could lead to disaster. So, I told her that I was not. "Are you Christian?" Well, at least I might redeem myself in her eyes by admitting to this. It was the opening she required and despite the fact that her evangelism was unsuccessful, we were able to have a cogent debate about religion with me plumbing the depths of my memory to access bible study from my Sunday school days.

Later she drove me back to the Hotel Ukraine and told me that she would meet me in the foyer at 08.30. I pushed my way through the much increased throng of willing ladies and reached my room ignoring the offers of the babooshka at the desk at the end of my corridor to "make arrangements" for me.

At 08.30 I found Livia easily in the much depopulated foyer. We walked over to the Ministry building but instead of climbing the intimidating steps, now almost devoid of guards; she led me around to the back of the building. There was an enormous queue which trailed back towards the far corner of the building. "What are they waiting for?" I asked. "The English School" she said. There at the head of the queue were two guards shepherding people into the building through this back door. Inside there were staff sitting at a table taking money from the intending students. It was incredible! These Foreign Affairs staff were moonlighting, running a private language school in their offices which were empty on Saturdays. I saw a couple of classes before we had lengthy negotiations about the recruitment of teachers from the UK for their "school" and the possibility of sending students to us.

Next day, on my way to the airport I found myself wondering. How on earth did this extraordinary enterprise find out about me and our school? Why us when there are other much better known and bigger organisations to turn to? I still do not know the answer.

We were fortunate enough to attend several language fairs in Russia in the mid nineties. This was a period when things in Moscow in particular, were very much in a state of flux. There was a feeling of the Wild West about the City. There were many business opportunities for those entrepreneurs brave enough to exploit them. But there was also a feeling of danger. Westerners were being kidnapped for ransom and there was much talk of turf wars among criminal underworld figures. We were lucky enough to have met a Russian lady, Natasha, in Salisbury who was married to a local man but who ran a travel business in Moscow. She acted as our minder and guide when we attended the language fairs. She booked us into the Hotel Moscow.

This hotel was an incredible place of vast proportions where previously Communist Party officials were put up in rooms which were in direct proportion in size to the importance in the Party of the occupant. It had been built partly with marble and stone from the Cathedral of Christ the Saviour. (This cathedral was consecrated in 1883 although it had originally been planned by Tsar Alexander 1 in 1812 to celebrate the victory over Napoleon. In December 1931, Stalin ordered the Cathedral to be dynamited to clear a site for a new Palace of Soviets. It took over a year to clear the site but because of a lack of funding and problems with flooding, the Palace was never built.).

Natasha had arranged a suite for us. Although it was large, indeed very large, with several rooms, it was austere with unattractive décor and acres of dark wooden panelling. The water heating system was antiquated and it was not long before we learnt to race our colleagues at the Fair back to the hotel each afternoon in order to be sure of enough hot water to shower. We realised when we checked out, that the previous occupants of the rooms during the recent Communist era must have not been above a bit of petty pilfering. There was a house rule that before leaving the hotel, a member of staff would come to do a stock take of all the engraved cutlery and glasses, (which included some very fine champagne glasses), in the suite lounge before the guest was allowed to leave.

It seemed a safe enough place, but Natasha insisted that we never answered a knock at the hotel room door, (she checked up on us by knocking on the door herself and if we opened it, pretended to shoot us!) and most importantly, that we took separate taxis from the hotel to the Fair and that the registration numbers of the taxis were noted and given to colleagues just in case of kidnap.

The language fairs themselves were, initially, a very questionable investment. The early ones were for the general public, the vast majority of whom did not have funds to pay for courses in the UK. But there were some who did. One afternoon a very well dressed gentleman drew me aside from our stand and asked if I was interested in a business proposal. As that is what I was there for I said I was.

"I want you to buy property for me in the United Kingdom" he growled at me. "If you can do this for me and my friends, you will be very well rewarded." As far as I could see there was nothing illegal about the proposal, this was long before the days with concerns regarding money laundering and so I did not decline to help him, but asked for more information.

"Later I will bring two hundred and fifty thousand US dollars for you to invest for us". Now it was getting serious, and I realised that though the proposal might not be illegal, the source of the money probably was. I hastily backtracked and said that I needed time to consider his proposal, could we meet tomorrow? Later, when I mentioned this proposal to Natasha she was near incandescent about the danger I was putting myself in. The man did not come back to me the next day and the last I saw of him was when he was in conversation with another exhibitor. Perhaps someone else helped him, perhaps he is very rich, perhaps he is dead.

As I mentioned earlier, these early language fairs were of dubious business value as they were open to the general public many of whom, in fact it sometimes seemed the majority, only wanted to practise their English. Later Fairs were only open to Language Travel agents and these were much more fruitful financially. But I would not have missed these early fairs, they gave us an opportunity to come into contact with ordinary Russians, the people who our missiles had been pointed at for forty years, and indeed whose government's missiles had been pointing at us. It was a humbling experience. We met some really enthusiastic anglophiles, a few older visitors had been listening to the BBC World Service to learn English even in the bad old days when, had they been caught, they might have ended up in a gulag or even worse. It was incredibly touching to meet some people who had never in their lives spoken to a native English speaker and yet, by dint of dedicated study, were near fluent.

One of our colleagues from a school on the south coast had considerably more business acumen than we did. He realised that his brochures were, like ours, disappearing fast to visitors who were probably never going to be able to travel to England, but who wanted to get reading materials. He put a charge of one dollar on his brochures. The effect was amazing, people queued to buy them. When his brochures were all gone he sold the posters on his stand and finally the red, white and blue balloons he had decorated the stand with. As he stood there behind his bare stand it dawned on him that perhaps it might be illegal to export US dollars from Russia. The rumour at the Fair was that he bought a pair of oversize shoes and walked through the airport passport control on two large wads of dollars.

We too had what turned out to be a very lucky break, though ours was of a very different nature. One of the visitors to our stand introduced herself as the editor of a teacher's magazine. She dearly wanted to have a chance to visit England and to attend a school. She asked if we were prepared to barter a series of free adverts in her magazine against the cost of a two week course and accommodation. Although the sample magazine she showed us was very unpretentious by Western standards, we agreed. The editor had her course but we only got one single enquiry in response to the advertisements. That response led to a very long and happy business relationship with a remarkable man; it was a relationship which earned us well over a hundred thousand pounds.

This new business associate was Valery Chernodedov. He lived in a most remote town in northern Siberia and because of its remoteness the business potential did not look very promising. What we underestimated was this man's entrepreneurial flair. He was a French specialist who had worked in French speaking countries during the Communist era. I never asked the nature of his work and he never volunteered the information. At the fall of the Soviet Union he set up a school in his home town and a Russian-French translation bureau. This developed to include English. He obviously had wealthy contacts as very soon he was sending us summer course students from his town and the nearest major city, Irkutsk. His administration, honesty and reliability were infallible. I was delighted to see his translation business, based on the use of the internet, grow to gain him blue chip international clients who probably had no idea that he was running the concern from remote northern Siberia. On three occasions he invited teachers, Pamela White, Martin Goddard and Rob McCall, from our School to spend a period teaching in his school. They were well looked after and had celebrity status there while experiencing a Siberian winter.

There was an air of excitement about Russia in the mid nineties; there was a new found freedom for the masses, though not necessarily wealth. Indeed the poor were very evident. Yet there was a buzz created by the birth of the new capitalism. I asked Natasha why, when it was patently dangerous to work in Moscow, she did not return to Salisbury. She explained that in the relative chaos and lawlessness of city life, which she hoped would only be temporary, there were amazing business opportunities and she wanted to be part of it. Life was certainly full of surprises.

I was alone in my hotel room at the end of the last day of a language fair where I had been representing the School by myself and was looking forward to a dinner with colleagues in a restaurant noted for catering for the festive demands of expatriate businessmen, when the telephone rang. I thought that it would be one of the usual calls, but it was instead the receptionist. She told me that I had some visitors waiting to see me in the hotel lounge. I assumed that some of my colleagues had decided to meet early for a drink. I had not had time to change and was still in my suit, but I went down to the reception desk.

I asked the receptionist where my visitors were and she called to a fellow who, though he looked like a heavyweight boxer, was immaculately dressed in a dark suit. He beckoned me towards the lounge and led me to a large sofa. On the sofa was another dark-suited well-built man, somewhat older than the first, but what really caught my eye was the fact that he sat next to a woman literally dripping with jewellery. She was elegant, very well dressed and possessed a well-coiffured head of dark hair. She looked very serious, indeed worried. Next to her squeezed in at the end of the sofa, was smartly dressed girl of about sixteen. Behind the sofa, at each end were two dark-suited men with their hands together held in front of them.

"Mr Wills?" quizzed the man on the sofa with a stentorian voice. "Yes", I said rather tremulously. He struggled up from his sitting position and one of the men behind the sofa leapt forward to help him. My hand disappeared into his bear-like paw. "We are pleased to meet you. This is my wife". He waved a hand towards the woman who had not reacted, so I guessed that she did not speak English. "And this is my daughter Julia." The girl did react and smiled shyly.

He made a hand signal to the man who had brought me in, to fetch an armchair. Judging by the ease with which he lifted it he was not employed solely for his brain. I sat down while the three on the sofa eyed me keenly.

"You have a school?" he asked. I agreed that I did. "Tell us about it."

I launched into the patter which had been well practised in the last three days of the Fair. He stopped me from time to time and translated for his wife. Occasionally his daughter asked him a question which he then posed to me. At this stage of course I really did not know what his interest was with me, I hoped that it was that he wanted his daughter to attend the School and not his henchmen.

At length, after interrogating me about Salisbury and how dangerous the City was he said, "I want my daughter to study at your school for one year. You will look after her like your own daughter. Great care must be taken. Now you will arrange a visa."

It was a dilemma. The possibility of a one year student with no expense spared, they had not even asked about the price! But what if she turned out to be difficult, I might find myself to have given Barbro at the very least a new teenage daughter to worry about, at worst a teenage tear away whose antics could result in a reckoning for me from this hefty bunch. My hunger for business overcame my fear of possible retribution. I asked if I could spend a few minutes alone with Julia to talk to her and ascertain her level of English and make some judgement about her motivation. She was totally charming and once away from the domination of her bear-like father, quite forthcoming. I went back to the sofa and asked to be excused to go to my room to collect some visa application forms.

When I came back the two men who had been standing behind the sofa had disappeared. I sat down and we worked our way through the forms. When we came to the section about nationality I discovered that my new friends were not Russian at all, but Georgian. The same nationality as Stalin I thought. We completed the forms and a school application form, the father gave me a cash deposit of a thousand dollars and I issued a letter of authority for the visa. I never did this lightly because the School would fare badly if we misused our authority to support visa applications. However, I could see no reason why the girl should not be granted a visa.

This was going to be a fine story to tell my colleagues at dinner I thought! I collected together all the papers and made to take my farewells.

"You will take your papers to your room and then we will eat," instructed the father.

Clearly this was not an invitation to be declined. By this stage I felt safe with these people, I could provide something they wanted and my well being was in their interest. I dashed up to my room dropped off the papers and tucked the cash into my money belt.

On returning downstairs I found the party milling around the entrance and suddenly realised that far from dining in the relative safety of the hotel restaurant they planned to go out. Oh thought I, no turning back at this point, so I consigned myself to the care of the Georgian Godfather. The mother, daughter, father, one henchman and I went through the doors and immediately two identical recent model black Mercedes cars drove up the ramp and stopped in front of us. I recognised the drivers as the two men who had previously been standing behind the sofa. I was ushered into the first car with the father and Julia. Her mother, together with their minder got into the car behind. I had no idea where we were heading and soon lost my bearings. I asked a few desultory questions about things and places we passed. Unlike many people I have never learnt to enjoy silence in company, often a dangerous weakness I admit. The other car stayed close behind us even when we were near to going through red lights.

Eventually we stopped outside a large shop front which did not immediately look like a restaurant. The driver jumped out and opened the door for us to get out and the whole party went into the restaurant together, abandoning the cars outside. I seriously doubt whether this would be possible in modern Moscow with current levels of traffic, but then it was and I realised that it was an ostentatious display of wealth to diners and passers by.

Inside the bustling Georgian restaurant, my new friend was treated with considerable reverence by the manager and we were shown past the diners' tables. Many heads turned and conversation dropped, some greeted the father. I noted that some of the tables appeared to be raised above floor level and I was later told that the level of the table denoted status. We were led up some stairs to a table which overlooked the whole restaurant and one could not avoid noticing that we were to a large extent on display to the assembled lower ranks of diners. Soon after, some Georgian musicians started playing and the noise level increased significantly as people raised their voices to be heard.

I was seated next to the father and opposite Julia. The atmosphere became much more relaxed, dangerously so as the very heavy Georgian wine flowed. I remember little of the meal, but there were many courses. However, I won my spurs as an honorary Georgian when a particular course was presented. In a huge tray filled with steaming brown gravy there were some large meatballs.

"Mr Wills, do you like bulls eggs?"

The whole table was observing me. The heady wine must have slowed my brain and I did not catch on. All watched as I was served two large meat balls, the father beckoned to the waiter to give me another. I scraped the rich gravy off one of the balls and realised immediately what they were, bull's testicles. Not wishing to give offence and not being aware of Georgian restaurant etiquette I slowly demolished the first one to the great amusement of my merry table fellows. Their attention to my plate made me realise that this foreigner was the butt of a joke. I was determined to eat for England, no difficulty for me normally. Amusement gave way to admiration after number two and finally to astonishment after the final one, by which time half of the restaurant were aware that a foreigner had met the challenge of the "bulls eggs". That done, I declined the offer of a sweet and I dreaded what effect my gluttony would have on me before tomorrow's journey. But the party went on until the small hours and eventually one of the drivers, who had certainly not stinted on wine consumption, drove me back to the hotel.

Julia duly came to Salisbury. She was an excellent student, responsible and well behaved. When she applied for a visa for another six months the visa application was refused. This was inexplicable and typical of the whims of the Entry Clearance Officers in Moscow. However, father was not to be hoodwinked by the vagaries of the UK authorities. He bought a house in Greece, took out dual Greek and Georgian nationality for his family and thus, since Greece had joined the European Union in 1981, Julia did not need a visa to travel to England.

Ukraine

In September 1995, Barbro and I took part in the first Language Fair in Kiev since Ukrainian independence in August 1992. It was a fascinating prospect and we made sure that we had a couple of extra days free at the end of the Fair to make the most of this opportunity to see as much of Kiev as possible.

Through the Fair organisers we had arranged to have a translator at our stand, but when we got there we found that we had two, a young man and a woman. My annoyance at the prospect of extra expense was quickly tempered when we had had a brief chat. They were a couple and they were prepared to share the fee. Over the three days of the fair we got

Our guides in Kiev. In the distance, the statue referred to below

to know them well, they were charming and enriched our understanding of the country greatly when they also volunteered to act as City guides for us.

We stayed in what we were told was one of the best hotels in Kiev. Our room overlooked a large square and though we first thought that it would suffer from traffic noise, it did not. There was hardly any traffic. There were very few private cars and the lorries and buses disappeared at night. Breakfast was our first adventure. We all queued with our trays and joined a snake of would-be diners winding round partitions at various counters where very stern faced ladies in white overalls served a standard breakfast. While it was possible to reject the offer of certain items, it was strictly forbidden to exceed the ration. One of my colleagues took a second boiled egg and the overalled guard clipped his hand with a wooden spoon.

Dinner was a proletarian affair. We learnt after the first day to anticipate the six o'clock dinner gong and get into line at the servery early. In true socialist fashion all the staff ate with the guests. On our fist night we found ourselves in the queue with cooks, doormen, receptionists and other staff all lined up in front of us taking the choicest items on display.

The Fair was very much like the first ones we had attended in Moscow. It was open to the public and once again we found ourselves providing English language practice to hundreds of highly motivated people who had no means to attend courses in the UK. However, they did not all lack enterprise. One lady came to our stand and through our translators we learnt that she was called Lydia and came from the north of the country. Her husband had given her a lift on his bicycle to get to the nearest station to travel to Kiev. She wanted to barter her homemade wall tapestries for a course in England for her daughter. Well, there are times when it is very difficult to let commercial sense dictate decisions. She showed us pictures of her designs and the one completed tapestry she had with her. We agreed and chose three designs to be made for us. Further we suggested that we could arrange for her tapestries to be exhibited in an art centre in Salisbury. To be honest I did not see how we would be able to get a UK entry visas for her daughter as the family had very little money, but we did. However, this scheme worked out to be much more expensive for us than we had calculated when, unexpectedly, the mother and a son turned up at the School with her daughter. They were penniless, how they got visas I do not know, but we supported them financially until they left the country. The three Ukrainian tapestries now adorn our walls.

Our two translators, both of whom were university students, were keen rock climbers. We were somewhat mystified when they told us that they financed their studies by climbing in Kiev. We had noticed that above the doorways of many of the buildings in the centre of Kiev there were metal pipes sticking out of the walls and wire netting stretched between them. We learnt that through neglect during the communist era, many of the fine old buildings in the City centre had crumbling facades. There had been several fatalities when brick work had fallen on to pedestrians in the streets.

The City Council had decided that the task of repairing all the buildings would take such a long time that some of them would have to be patched up while waiting for a more thorough repair. A team of rock climbers had been recruited to scale these dangerous buildings to remove loose masonry and where possible to patch up cracks with cement.

Our young friends gave us many other interesting insights into the way of life in the country. They introduced us to one man who told us about the Chernobyl atomic power station disaster in April 1986. He said that after the explosion, loudspeaker vans toured the City telling people to stay indoors, but no information was given about the nature of the danger for over a week. He told us that the only precaution they were told to take by the authorities was to hose down the pavements. The Pripyet River flows past Chernobyl and joins the Dneiper which flows through Kiev. Although radioactive sludge still contaminated the river bed when we were there, the banks of the river in the City were lined with anglers looking for a fish supper.

Our climbing friends showed us with pride a huge statue which had been built in honour of a visit from Brezhnev. It was an enormous figure carrying a golden sword. However, their pride was not in the statue itself but in the fact that the sword was truncated. Apparently, the top of the original sword was higher than the pinnacle of the highest building in Kiev, the Great Lavra Bell Tower. This gave great offence to the Ukrainian nationalists. Our friends' climbing club had launched a nocturnal raid on the statue and at considerable height had sawn off three metres of the sword to reduce the height to below that of the Tower.

Unfortunately, the couple misjudged my enthusiasm for heights. They showed us around several of the fantastic churches in the City and finally we went to St Sophia's Cathedral. As climbers they had permission to go right up inside the highest dome at the top of the Cathedral. The place was accessed first by good solid steps, but further up by wooden ladders. We were coaxed up to a viewing platform underneath the top dome, which gave a fantastic view of the City, but at a height which terrified me. I found myself holding tight to anything solid while the two of them jauntily sat on the narrow parapet describing the view.

On our final day we were taken to Pyrohiv, south of Kiev. Our guides had borrowed a car which would not have looked out of place in a motor museum and we rattled and jolted our way to the Museum of Folk Architecture and Life of Ukraine. We were surprised to see it was called "Skansen". This is the name of the area in Stockholm where there is also an outdoor museum. There was a fascinating collection of wooden buildings, including churches, from all over the country, spread over a one and a half kilometre site.

This visit to the Ukraine eventually gave us some good business but the rewards from this particular visit could not be counted in money. We learnt a lot about a proud nation in a corner of Europe seldom visited by the British and we made one lady very happy; we still have the tapestries.

St Sophia's Cathedral

Our visits to these ex-Soviet countries so soon after the cataclysmic events of 1989 gave us a unique opportunity to observe and enjoy the celebration of freedom of these millions of people who in most cases had lived under one or other form of cruel dictatorship for the whole of their lives, not just in the Soviet satellite countries but in Russia itself.

Italy

Despite the fact that in our final years at SSE our Spanish market rivalled the Italian one, there is no doubt that historically the School's success was due in no small measure to the loyalty of our Italian clients who came year after year. As I write elsewhere, our first group business was with Carlo Sigismondi and this was quickly followed by an amazingly successful series of courses arranged for two Italian ladies, Rosa Pugliesi and Marisa Balzarini. Indeed so successful, that Marisa brought us groups for 25 years in succession, sometimes twice a year. These contacts were initially passed to us by the late Nick McIver, to whom I am eternally grateful.

Marisa Balzarini

In 1982 an old teacher colleague from my time in Sweden, Tricia Hedge, recommended us to one of her co-authors on a writing project, Deanna Donatini. After trying a course with us, Deanna recommended us to a fledgling educational travel agent called Incontri Europei. This contact gave us two things, a wonderful Italian friend at the agency and our most substantial volume of Italian business over 28 years (the last two being at our Weymouth Centre, after we had sold SSE). Incontri's business grew in step with our organisation and I am pleased to say that its subsidiary, New Beetle is now a major Italian educational travel company.

I have covered a lot of years in two paragraphs above. What I have not said was that I made several other early attempts to create Italian business. My first was in 1982 when an Italian teacher who had attended one of our teachers' courses asked if we would run a week's course in Milan to train Italian teachers of business English. I had never even been to Italy so the challenge was very exciting. I hoped to pick up a number of Italian teacher contacts, to see something of the country and of course the extra income for the School would be useful. I took with me a very successful business English teacher, ME, with whom I would share the training. (Unfortunately, I later had to sack this very pleasant lady for stealing our one-to-one students in Salisbury and teaching them privately at home!).

The course went very well apart from an incident concerning room sharing in the adult learning centre where the course was run. One day, a priest who was running a course in the same building had to yield to the tumult when my course participants found that he had taken over one of our classrooms where we had set up video cameras and other paraphernalia. When he saw me he shouted something at me in Italian. I asked a teacher what he had said.

"Go to hell!" she replied. For once I managed a reply which could silence even an Italian. Say to him "I'll see you there!" I asked of the teacher. The effect was dramatic. He barged past robes flowing and never troubled us again.

At the end of the week ME's gentleman friend, a real charmer called Jack who drove a Rolls Royce at home, arrived to join her for a long weekend. Barbro also arrived for her first taste of Italy.

We had been invited to visit the home of our Italian one-to-one student, and by now good friend, Andrea Cecchi. He had arranged for his father, Luigi (alas no longer with us), to drive us from Milan to Tuscany. Mr Cecchi, a giant of a man in every sense, duly collected us from our hotel on Friday evening at the end of the course. It transpired that he was President of the Italian Wine Growers Association and had been attending a meeting in Milan. It was completely dark and so we saw nothing of the countryside as we made frighteningly fast progress southwards. We stopped once near Parma where he warned me not to try the local wine, Lambrusco, as it was dreadful and he regarded it only a fizzy drink.

Villa Cerna. From left to right, Andrea, Aunt Anna, Mrs Cecchi, and Cesare

The last part of the journey was up a steep country road at the top of which was a pair of very stately iron gates. Luigi opened them electronically and we drove through to a large courtyard in front of a substantial building, this was Villa Cerna. Andrea, his mother and his aunt were standing in the doorway to welcome us and we were ushered into a cavernous room with vaulted ceilings and fine furnishings. It was all a bit overwhelming and of course we were well tired, but the welcome was so wonderful and genuine that we were quite moved. After some refreshment which naturally included some of their best Chianti Classico we retired to our bedroom suite. The next morning stands out for me, and I am sure for Barbro, as one of the most memorable of our lives.

We were woken by what sounded like a child screaming under our window. Soon there was a chorus of these most dreadful screams. And then it stopped, as if the producers of the sound had had their lives terminated. We threw open the wooden shutters and were totally spellbound by the magnificent sight of the sun shining over mile after mile of absolutely straight rows of green vines climbing the surrounding undulating hills. Glancing down we could see that the source of the earlier commotion was a flock of peacocks which had just been fed.

We spent three days at this magnificent place enjoying the comfort of the Villa, learning about wine production and enjoying the true friendship of wonderful people.

Not all of my forays to Italy were spent in such luxury! Indeed my next visit was just the opposite. I do not know how she learnt about the School but M.S. asked for us to arrange a course in Italy. I had never met her before, but I learned later that she had been a minor opera star who had washed up in Italy and had decided to start a small language school in Mantova. I was to learn too, that even minor opera stars can be major prima donnas.

As part of the launching of the school she had planned two activities. Firstly, for the most influential movers and shakers of Mantova an expensive wine tasting which was to be directed by a nationally famous sommelier and secondly, a free business English course for the top executives of the biggest employer in the area, a petro-chemical complex called Montipolimeri. M.S. wished to contract me to teach the latter.

I saw this as an opportunity to use the new school as a "feeder" to get students to Salisbury and also I thought that there might be an opportunity to get company business from Montipolimeri. I agreed terms with M.S. but I was not happy about the invitation to stay in her flat to minimise accommodation costs. However, I agreed and carefully planned the course. I insisted on having test results showing the language level of the students, and a statement called a Needs Analysis where the prospective students indicate their perceived language training needs. I was blissfully unaware that most of the executives got their secretaries to fill in both!

The course got off to a good start even so, although my reliance on adjusting the second input session of the day with the experience gained during the first session was torpedoed when the company coffee break turned out to be the time it takes to swallow an espresso!

However, I was not happy with the accommodation arrangement. Apart from the tedium of listening to my hostess doing scales with a voice which could have cracked a flower pot, I had her bedroom while she slept elsewhere in the flat. I think that she had quickly realised that she was not going to add me to her male conquests and told me the second evening that she had invited Signor F, a most influential man in the town to call on her the following evening. If this was to make me jealous it had the opposite effect, it presented me with a chance to make alternative arrangements. Her new classrooms in an adjoining building were newly decorated and as yet unused. In addition there was a shower room in the building. I suggested that if she could arrange a camp bed for me I would gladly leave the field open for Snr F.

Thus, on Wednesday I decamped to the classroom. My relief was tempered by the fact that I had overlooked that there were no curtains. There was also the fact that the smell of the carpet-layer's glue which I had noticed earlier had not been dissipated by the passing of time as I had thought it would be. The camp bed was little more than a stretcher with legs, but still I rejoiced in my new found independence. I had several chairs and the classroom tables for company and settled for my first night in these new quarters. I decided to read for a while before bed as I could not read in bed without the full illumination of the classroom lights betraying my residential status to all the neighbouring flats. The word would no doubt go round that I had been evicted by my hostess! It would be a wonder to them what felony I had been guilty of to have been cast out of her house.

I turned out the lights and undressed in the light of the lamppost outside. As I descended to the level of the awaiting camp bed I became acutely aware that the offending glue fumes must be heavier than air as the smell was much more intense at low altitude. I lay in bed worrying about the possibility that the odiferous compound might cause brain damage. Eventually, I fell asleep whether by dint of tiredness or the anaesthetic effect of the smell I know not.

Neither was the smell better in the morning and I had certainly not become oblivious to it. I dressed with the strong suspicion that I was providing breakfast entertainment for the residents of the flats across the road and went off to break my fast at the local café. On returning from work that evening I decided that something had to be done about the glue problem. I opened all the classroom windows. I would have to close them at night, but in the shower room there was a window high up above the toilet which had the appearance of owning hinges and thus might be left open all night to provide fresh air.

I closed the toilet lid and mounted the slippery plastic cover. I gingerly lifted one foot to mount the top of the cistern, a position which once reached, would enable me to grasp a latch which I had seen on the window. Clearly, the designer of the lid had not anticipated such a use for his product. The lid gave way. There was a tremendous crash which must have been heard all down the street since the windows were open. One of my feet, shoe and all, went down the lavatory pan.

I tried to regain my composure and check if any of the numerous shards of plastic had lacerated my leg. All seemed to be well but I was trapped with one foot in a most unseemly place. I tried pulling and twisting my foot to get free but it is the nature of the orifice in which I was stuck that there was little room for objects of such dimension. I wondered if the terrible sound of the cracking lid might bring a posse of neighbours to my aid, but then decided that such humiliation would be unbearable and ceased immediately to hope for such deliverance.

My salvation depended on me alone. Further examination of the predicament indicated that if I could release the shoe lace I might be able to get my foot out of the shoe. No time to be squeamish. I delved deep into the water with both hands and managed to undo the bow, but the lace itself was still too tight. I spent what seemed an age tugging at the lace to loosen it as far down the shoe as I could reach before it was obstructed by the bend in the pan. Eventually, by dint of the adrenaline which flows in emergencies, I managed to slide my foot out and then recover my soggy shoe.

If any of my executives next day noticed that I was wearing suede shoes of different colour by virtue of one being wet, no one said anything. After the day's class I was to be seen standing at the check-in desk of the cheapest hotel in town, suitcase in hand waiting for a room to be assigned to me.

This experience did not put me off Italy, but I have not felt inclined to visit Mantova again. On later sales trips to the country I often took the family. We had by that time many good friends who loved to see the girls and were very hospitable to us. In order to make such outings financially possible we sometimes drove all the way. The most memorable such journey was in 1987 before the time when Sweden had joined the European Union.

We had taken the night boat to St Malo and arrived at 06.00 in the morning. Emma was but nine years old and Anna the oldest, fourteen. When we had driven off the boat a gendarme asked for our passports which were duly handed over. He walked away from us looking at the documents and then suddenly turned and rounded on me. "Ou est la Suedoise?" he demanded. I indicated that Barbro had that honour. He commanded in French that she should immediately leave the car. The children were quite terrified, as indeed I was, to see their mother marched away between two policemen. I got out to protest in best schoolboy French and was told by a third policeman that

Swedes needed a visa to travel in France. Presumably, by this time this had also been explained to Barbro. She turned to wave in a fruitless attempt to allay the children's fears as she was frog marched (no pun intended), up the gang plank and back on board the ship. I shouted to her to go to the French embassy in London and then fly out to Italy to meet us.

I returned to the car and suddenly realised the challenge which faced me. I had to drive alone to our destination north of Milan with the three children. I explained the situation to them and we agreed to go on rather than go back to England. However, just as we were about to leave, a gendarme walked up to the car and banged on the roof. I opened the window and he leant towards me in a conspiratorial fashion. He held up his thumb and forefinger and rubbed them against each other. He growled, "Monsieur, there is a way to solve this". My Anglo Saxon sense of ethics overcame my business sense (though it might have been cheaper to pay off the policeman than for Barbro to pay for a flight from England), and as impolitely as I dared, I told him to push off in the direction of a very hot place.

The children were allotted jobs, map reading, sorting change for the toll roads, keeping diaries and so on, and off we went. Sixteen hours later I pulled up outside a hotel in Chamonix and we stopped for the night. Next morning we set off and went through the Mont Blanc tunnel and down the beautiful Aosta Valley. At 16.30 when we arrived at our friends house in Buggugiate near Varese; they were delighted to see us and we them. But best of all, behind them stood Mrs Wills. She had got there before us having gone straight to London the day before to get a visa and then having flown to Milan that morning!

Salisbury was a popular destination for Italian students and many of them came back year after year. Neither was the traffic one way, several host families were invited to visit the homes of students in Italy. (We were not aware of how frequently this happened with all of our student nationalities; even long haul ones such as Japanese, until we retired).

In relation to the huge number of Italian students who attended the School over the years, we had very few difficulties. However, when things did go wrong they could be quite dramatic. Early on we had a few shoplifting cases, very few, but enough for us to develop a zero tolerance approach. Any student arrested by the police would be sent home. The guilty ones always had money; they stole only for fun, that is, except those sad cases where there was a psychological reason.

In 1986 a young boy came to us for the second year running. We later learned that there had been some trouble at his host family during the first year regarding things disappearing, but the family liked the boy so much that they did not mention anything to us. The boy's parents were effusive in their thanks about the boy's first stay and had sent us a present of silk, for they were in that trade.

Early on in the boy's second stay things started going missing from the bags of the students in his class. By a process of elimination we were able to deduce that he was the likely culprit. On Friday I called him to my room and searched his bag. To my horror it was bulging full of packeted small goods from shops, a melted ice cream, and various effects which other students had said that they had lost. He immediately admitted that he had taken the items from other students and various shops.

I sent the boy outside to wait while I considered what to do. I could not easily send an unaccompanied 13 year-old home. As it happened, the difficulty was solved for me. I called Barbro to advise me as this was a welfare issue. She came in with a copy of a telex we had just received which told us in English that the boy's mother would be arriving on Saturday morning to see her son. We knew that she did not speak English, so someone must have written it for her.

Next morning, I was in my office, Italian phrase book on my desk, waiting for the mother to arrive, the boy was at home with his host family. A ring at the door bell and there was a lady who could only be Italian, carrying two parcels. In very, very halting English she said that she was the lad's mother and she had brought presents for me and Barbro. This was excruciatingly embarrassing. I realised that she did not have the English to understand my explanation of the situation and the poor lady was bearing gifts for us. I took her into my office and laboriously started to explain in simple English and very poor Italian that her son must leave. It was a horrible situation, but as soon as I showed her her son's bag she understood completely. He had clearly done this before and I later realised that the poor lady had hoped that a different environment might cure him of his serious kleptomania. By midday the two of them were heading for the airport and I had a silk tie for me and a bolt of silk on my desk for Barbro.

She was not the last parent we came into contact with who had hoped that a child's psychological difficulties might be cured by a stay in England. The most spectacular of these were the French girl who had visions of writhing snakes around her bedroom and the Swedish boy who smashed up a telephone box in the market square in full view of the CCTV cameras and then stood by the wreckage waiting for the police to arrest him in order to satisfy his need for attention.

We had thousands of Italian students and only once was there a case of drunkenness, but it was on a grand scale! By the year 2000 we had a well established winter teenage course season. At the beginning of January the year opened with our South American "Summer School", then at the end of February our Japanese agent usually sent a large group of girls from a private school in Tokyo. In March and April we often got "closed" Italian groups. That is, students from a particular Italian school class who were not mixed internationally at SSE but taught in their own classes, often with a particular educational objective related to their Italian school curriculum. These groups were normally led by their own school teachers, the vast majority of whom were pleased to be in the UK, made the most of the opportunity and were a pleasure for us to deal with. A small minority were in England under sufferance!

One of the latter persuasion, a male teacher, seemed to pay little attention to his students' welfare and spent most of his time in the City pubs rather than attending and supporting the evening events which we had arranged for his students.

One very wet Friday evening in March I received a desperate sounding phone call from Bill, the Social Activities Manager, to say that half the Italian students had not turned up at the appointed time for a disco he had arranged for them. I tried unsuccessfully to reach the Italian leader for support. Half an hour later we had a phone call from the police to say that a member of the public had called them to report that they had found a foreign girl face down in the gutter in Crane Street and that a patrol was attending.

At this point I should say that such was the influence on the City of SSE that it was often assumed by the police that any foreigner, child or adult who they came across would be one of our students. This sometimes led to us assisting the police with translators and advice for foreigners who had nothing to do with the School. Unfortunately, on this occasion the report was very much to do with us.

A little later we received a second call from the police to say that they had two Italian girls at the station in the grandly named "custody suite". One was completely drunk and had passed out and the other, who seemed to be completely sober, had been able to give them personal details. The police had also rounded up two other drunken Italian students who were in a police car waiting outside the School building for someone to collect them.

Clearly we could not send them home to their host families in such a state. Barbro headed off for the school to set up a field hospital to try to sober up the children, while I went to the police station to decide what was to be done with the comatose girl.

At the police station I was quickly ushered into the custody suite. It was quite a modern series of cells along a subterranean corridor at the end of which was a desk. Behind this a burly looking policeman was trying to persuade a handcuffed middle-aged man to stop shouting. Nor were the cell doors sound proof, there was much banging on them and cursing emanating from behind them. One of the cell doors was open and inside was a supine female on a plastic covered bed and a woman police officer sitting with a clip board talking to a girl I recognised as one of our students. A long conversation with the WPC ensued with frequent interruptions occasioned by the arrival of new miscreants to the suite. I requested that the girl should be taken to hospital but was told that they were waiting for the arrival of a police doctor to get advice on the best course of action.

This was clearly no place for a sixteen year-old girl to linger so I arranged for the sober one of the two to be driven home in a police car. The other girl being completely oblivious of her surroundings stayed until soon after midnight when the police doctor pronounced her drunk but not in need of medical attention. The police clearly needed the cell for others and told me that I must remove her. The only thing for it was to take her to the School so that Barbro could supervise her rehabilitation. I was asked to sign a form taking responsibility for her and asked to bring my car round to the back of the police station to the entrance of the custody suite. I spread a blanket on the back seat just in case and a police officer carried her out and dumped her unceremoniously on it.

It is quite amazing how little attention motorists pay to the occupants of other cars. On three occasions on my journey to the School I stopped at traffic lights, well in the glare of street lighting, with other cars besides me. At each, I was acutely aware that I had what must appear to be a body on my back seat. No one paid any heed whatever.

On arrival at the School I could see that the lights were on, but I could not park directly outside as other vehicles were there. I stopped as near as I could and went to give Barbro the news that she had another patient. The problem was how to get the girl inside the building. I could certainly not carry her fifty metres to the School alone. Even getting her out of the car would be a major challenge. As always, Barbro had the best idea. We wrapped the blanket around the recumbent form and dragged her out to a position where I could hold one end of the blanket and Bill Jennings the other. We were completely ignored by the occasional dog walker and got the girl safely on to the floor in the ground floor classroom. The scene in the classroom was grim; there were now three girls and a boy sitting around the classroom table asleep, with their heads on their arms and several buckets containing the contents of their dinners.

And so it was that we spent most of the night. As each student showed signs of reviving sufficiently for us to feel reasonably confident that the host family would accept taking over responsibility, we called the families to come to collect them. The last to go was the late occupant of my car who by 03.00 was as bright as a daisy. We were not.

In the summer we always advertised the fact that in addition to our usual range of classes we had classes for adults who were complete beginners. Paradoxically, very few teachers were able to teach complete beginners. Doing so required techniques seldom needed when teaching students of reasonably well educated European origin.

However, we detected that there was some market demand and so we advertised beginners' classes for sound business reasons. Quite often a student with some English would ask if his or her partner who was a beginner could study too. This was usually a condition of the more proficient student coming. At other times, we had the grotesque situation of people lying about their level of English just so that we would accept them as part of a group.

Generally speaking the only real beginners in Europe were those of a generation which either learnt German as a first foreign language early on, for example, many older Swedes were in this category, or those of a generation when there were schools which did not teach a foreign language.

Thus it was that we got two summer enrolments from a pair of adult Italians, who were enrolled as part of a small teenagers group. The enrolment form was scrappily filled in but we gleaned their names and address as well as the fact that the woman was 79 and the man 69, and that they were beginners.

Most Monday mornings I sought the refuge of my office on the first floor of Fowlers Road. The welcoming team headed up by Barbro did a better job when I was not around interfering with duties which I had delegated. Later in the morning my managers and Barbro would report on the new arrivals and any issues which needed to be addressed by me. So, I did not actually witness the moment when our Italian beginners graced the entrance to the School, but details were related to me by those present. I was however, later in the day, able to confirm the vivid descriptions of the appearance of the two.

The frantic job of welcoming new arrivals on a busy summer Monday morning came to a halt when the couple came through the door. He was wearing a dark suit and tie, nothing worthy of note there apart from the unnecessary formality, but the lady caused the Monday morning hubbub to hush. I will call her Carmen, although she was Italian and not Spanish it is a name she was deserving of.

Following, in two flouncing steps behind her partner, whose function appeared to be to part the crowds so that Carmen's full splendour could be observed, she entered with a flourish of the coloured handkerchief in her right hand. She wore high heels and a dress the length of which exposed a fine pair of legs. And what a dress! I do not remember the colour, only the flashing of the sparkling sequin reflectors in horizontal rows. The extravagant sartorial display was set off by a carefully groomed head of black hair which was crowned by a comb keeping a red rose in place.

The throng of new and returning students milling in the reception parted to allow the couple to announce themselves. Fortunately, we had an Italian speaker on the staff and we were able to make them welcome in their own language. Like all new students they were then taken to the student lounge to await the induction process.

It was not long before Barbro was in my office to report on the new intake and to warn me that we might have a couple of eccentrics on our hands. As soon as she had left I heard the knock on my door which I recognised, and expected. The Director of Studies had a phobia about beginners and always sought comfort from me when they materialised.

He waved their entrance tests at me and bemoaned the fact that they were only able to fill in their names. No surprise in that I told him with the tone of an officer trying to put backbone in his men. However, his next statement did floor me. Jane, (our Italian speaker), had talked to them and they had asked when the dancing was going to start. They said they had enrolled for the Disco Dance class.

Through the day the magnitude of the challenge became clear. The Italians had somehow picked up a copy of our Teenage Course brochure in Italy and had seen that we had classes in Disco

Dance for students. What they had not understood was that not only were these classes for teenagers and only twice a week, but that what our School primarily did was to teach English. Thus it was, we had on our hands two very, very mature dance addicts, helpless as lambs with no English and no plans or motivation to learn any either. We had only one option and that was to run a little class for them for two weeks.

The teacher took them on trips and generally kept them occupied until their big moment came when they joined the bi-weekly teenagers Disco Dance class. In fact, despite the pressure of looking after the social needs of five hundred other students, our ever inventive Social Activities Manager, Bill, was able to provide some other opportunities for the couple to display their dancing prowess, on the adult social programme. Unfortunately, Carmen deserted the English class in the second week, we have no idea what she did with herself, but we had to continue to tie up a much needed member of staff to keep her dance partner occupied.

We had quite a lot of business from southern Italy including Sicily. It was on a visit to attend a business meeting that I had an unwelcome brush with the Mafia.

In the eighties and early nineties I was a member of the local Rotary club and one year I was appointed international secretary. This job entailed arranging the annual international evening. I chose an Italian theme and arranged for the promotions director of a large Italian tourist organisation, based in London, to give an illustrated talk. After the talk I entertained the gentleman to dinner, no great hardship as he was very amiable and good company. We got on well and arranged that next time I was in London on business we would meet for lunch.

Eventually, we had our lunch together. During the meal he confided in me that he was being blackmailed. Somehow, he had had an upset with a unionised employee of the agency. Subsequently, he had been visited by an acquaintance who had commiserated with him about the conflict with the employee mentioned and asked him his view of the person and the union involved. My Italian friend had been unwise enough to say exactly what he thought about both. A few days later he had received an audio cassette through the post with a recording of the latter conversation. There followed a demand for payment.

My friend realised that if his remarks were published in the Italian press he would lose his job. So, he paid to get the original tape. He never got it.

Shortly after, Barbro and I were travelling on a plane to Palermo to attend a business conference. In front of us was a very loud Italian man, much the worse for drink, who got louder as the flight continued. After a while he turned round, kneeling on his seat and attempted to converse with us.

"Why are you going to Palermo? He asked.

Not wishing to provoke him I told him.

"Aren't you afraid of the Mafia?"

"Why should I be?" I replied.

There was a silence and then he held up a cassette tape to me and said, "I am celebrating, I am taking this tape to my "family" we are blackmailing a man in a travel bureau in London. He is paying well."

I was completely stunned. It could only be my friend he was referring to. The situation was very unpleasant and this man was clearly telling me, very loudly, a lot more than he should. He had attracted a lot of attention by this time and fortunately, some other Italians told him to shut up. Reluctantly, he turned round and resumed his seat. But the whole experience was very disturbing.

China

Undoubtedly, the most interesting business trips we made were to China. We moved into the Chinese market quite soon after travel restrictions for Chinese going abroad were eased. This was partly because we found a very good business contact in Matthew Ffookes, an Englishman living in China, and partly because we had opportunities to accompany official, DTI sponsored, delegations from Southampton Council by virtue of the fact that we belonged to Southampton Chamber of Commerce.

However, my first visit to China in 1994 was very much a self designed affair. I had been contacted by a Finnish woman who was living with her husband in Beijing and asked if we could help a Chinese businesswoman friend called Liu, who wanted to start an agency sending students to England. The intention was for the students to study at EFL schools and then to move on to full time university education in the UK. Her difficulty was that she knew very little about the procedure to obtain visas. These ladies invited me to come to Beijing, meet prospective students and help them with their visa applications.

The visit duly took place. It was a steep learning curve. I had to find contacts at the British Council and the Consulate in Beijing so that I had some credibility in the eyes of these women, and familiarise myself with the arcane routines of the visa office. It was a successful visit in the sense that I did manage to get visas for two students and the attendant enrolments for the School, but it made me aware that we would have to do a lot of work in England establishing contacts with universities to provide a study path for these students.

I had some time for sightseeing. The women took me to the Great Wall by taxi. It was a hair raising journey. On the long straight stretches of road the driver insisted on driving on to the left carriageway. Every time he saw a vehicle approaching he swerved back to the right hand side. Eventually, I asked my companions to ask him why he was doing this. He replied that the road was smoother on the other side!

This first visit led to a series of later visits, each of them better organised than the one before as we established a wider network of agents.

In 2003 we arranged for my father to fly out to China to meet us there during a business trip. He was tremendously enthusiastic about everything Chinese and later gave illustrated talks about his visit, to various organisations. We had a fine time together and managed to cram in a visit to Xian to see the terracotta warriors and a day in the Forbidden City. Our guide and interpreter on this trip was Lilian, a university student, who became a great friend of dad's.

In 2004 we were fortunate enough to get an invitation to join an official Southampton delegation to Beijing, Qingdao and Shanghai. The other participants were largely export oriented business people who hoped to sell goods and services to China for the preparations for the Olympic Games in 2008, in particular, maritime services for the port of Qingdao where the sailing events would take place.

As this was an official visit it was quite formal, with banquets and official receptions. But we had plenty of opportunities to see existing and potential agents for the School. The main formal event was a visit to a new business park outside Beijing, where the Chairman of Southampton Council would be asked to perform the opening ceremony. This occasion turned out to be part farce and part salutary notice of the speed and determination of the Chinese to develop their economy. We were bussed through the city with a police outrider escort and out into the country. Eventually our guide told us that we were approaching the business park. We all craned to look out of the windows, but could see nothing apart from a very, very large field. We drove around a perimeter road and noticed that there were the remains of foundations here and there, where small buildings had been removed. Then we saw two hovels with a pig in a pen outside of each, which had so far eluded the demolishers. In one corner of the field was a huge new warehouse building which appeared to be in the final stages of construction. We continued round the field back to our starting point. There some workers were putting the finishing touches to a substantial wooden podium. This was flanked with Chinese flags and a union jack.

The place was dreadfully exposed and the strong wind was finding the parts of the red cloth covering the podium which had not been properly nailed down. The mud was keeping the long red carpet in place. A coach arrived and a band disembarked and put their instruments into order. Two more coaches appeared with the crowd who would be applauding the speeches.

The delegation was asked to take up position on the podium and a speech in Chinese was translated for us before the applause. TV cameras panned the crowd and the podium. The Chinese anthem was played by the band who obviously new it by heart, but when it came to playing God Save the Queen, the sheet music having blown away from some of the music stands, we were treated to an "unusual" version which just added to the general surrealism of the occasion. The Southampton Chairman made his speech, which was translated for the crowd. As the applause died down there was a loud bang, followed by an intensive firework display, much of which could not be seen because of the daylight.

The event having concluded we were driven back whence we had come by our generous hosts. A memorable occasion in every way, but it did serve to illustrate for us the scale on which the Chinese work. No doubt, within a short time the whole field would be covered by commercial enterprises and the fact that it had once been covered by the small holdings of peasant farmers, consigned to history.

The same official visit concluded in Shanghai with a visit to a night club arranged by our hosts. We were bussed out of the city to a barn of a place. There was a dance floor beside which a group was playing, an enormous bar and surrounding the whole building an indoor balcony from whence those not dancing could observe the goings on below. Barbro and I sat at a table with two high ranking officials of Southampton Council enjoying as relaxing drink. After a while three girls appeared at our table, obviously tasked with entertaining the men. One attempted to sit on the lap of the highest ranking official. Hugely embarrassed by this display of largess, he pushed the girl aside and turned his back on her. For some reason he was still wearing his duffle coat. He put up the hood and sat monk like, where any attempt by the unscrupulous to photograph him with the girl, would not succeed.

I did not move as quickly, a girl sat on my lap, and running her fingers through my hair, asked if I would buy her a drink. I responded saying that she should ask my wife who was sitting on the other side of the table. Totally unabashed, she continued to flirt with me.

"He has three daughters about your age!" blurted Barbro ineffectually.

She tried another tack.

"He is old enough to be your father!" she shouted over the noise of the music.

She asked me my age and repeated her request for a drink. It was no good, I had to be very unpleasant to get rid of her, a fact I felt bad about later because the deal was probably that she got commission on drinks. A lean evening for her.

On Dad's second visit to China in 2005, we were concerned about a ninety year-old travelling alone. Emma agreed to accompany him and we all met up in Hong Kong. Barbro and I had one more business appointment and this was in mainland China in Xiajiou, so Emma and Dad went with us. At the lunch banquet where we were regally entertained by our generous hosts, we sat at a circular table and were first served with soup. I looked into my bowl and saw some bits of meat and two small black lumps on one of the pieces. Meanwhile Dad, on the other side of the table, out of earshot, was tucking into his soup. I asked my host what kind of soup this was. "Snake soup", she replied. I realised that the two little black lumps were the eyes of the dead snake peering up at me. Dad was offered a second helping which he accepted with enthusiasm. I did not tell him what the soup had been until we returned to the UK!

Mrs Fanny and George of SEDA

Our final visit to China was in 2006. I wanted to brief our Chinese agents on the impending sale of our business and to ensure that they would continue to send students to Salisbury, while actively marketing Weymouth to agents who had not used SSE.

By this time we had really good business connections with a company in Shenzhen called SEDA. The owner, Mrs Fanny, was dependable, delightful and extremely well connected, an important fact when doing business in China. We had had a substantial amount of business from her in Weymouth. In order to consolidate her relations with her clients she asked that Barbro and I should go on a tour with one of her staff to promote Weymouth. She had arranged for us visit several schools, one of which was her major supplier of students.

Here are notes from my diary of this trip:

Monday 6/3/06 Hong Kong

Taxi to the station, plenty of willing helpers. B. only just managed to close the suitcases, now with all her purchases. Easy train ride to Low Won and then walked over the bridge to Mainland China.
14.15 met up with Elliner the Shenzhen agent representative. Rain and very hot. Car to the airport and then 17.45 plane to Wuhan. A noodle feast before takeoff. Good flight, arrived 19.15 and took taxi to Hotel Asia. Wuhan is a mix of dilapidation and modernity with the scales tipped in the direction of the former. We met the Principal of the school with a gift of a tray of cherries transported by Elliner.
It is warm - probably 24C - and humid. Clearly we are in a high-pressure area as all the fumes are captured and the air is palpably grey. A sweaty night.

Tuesday 7/3/06

At 11.45 we went to nearby restaurant to meet teachers of School 11, some of whom I had met last year. A challenging lunch, lots of questions and I am very unclear about the hierarchy in the party and who has to gain face. 15.15 off to No 11 School, gave audio visual presentation of Weymouth to 160 children.
18.00 went to see Wu river and had a bizarre dinner including ducks' tongues and chicken feet fritters. Very bad night – so hot.

Wednesday 8/3/06

Alarm at 05.45, breakfast in room. Taxi to station the size of which would dwarf Wembley. Taxi stopped 300 m. short because of traffic. We have very heavy suitcases. Exhausting fighting through the crowds to get to waiting room number 4 in the heat. " Room" is too diminutive a term for the cavernous aircraft hanger- like building, absolutely packed with people and baggage. Redolent of a scene from Exodus. When train K7 came in at 08.00 the scene looked like a seething mass of humanity rushing from a natural disaster. In Hall No 4 we had been prize exhibits, clearly it was very unusual for Europeans to be here. Elliner commented that they looked at us as if we are from Mars. Heck of a crush on the train but we have numbered places. Having got on the train and found seats the heat became intense. Non seat holders stood or sat on the floor. B felt unwell, I realised she had the bug I had had and I remembered too how it had debilitated me, aided by the heat and humidity. B fainted and then was violently sick over herself and to a lesser extent me. Passengers scattered and we tried to clear up, but not very successfully. Elliner rushed for the attendant and returned to say that she had made arrangements for B to get changed and that we could sit in the restaurant car. We did a deal with a couple to take our seats if the man helped with carrying B's suitcase forward. It was a huge struggle to get through 2 carriages full of people standing or sitting on the floor, with the luggage. In the restaurant car the air was better but we had to keep pecking at food for the next 4½ hours to keep our seats. At each stop more people got on the train, most of the travellers were going to Dalian, a 28-hour journey – the conditions in the carriages were incredibly cramped and hot. Eventually we reached Zhengzhou. We slugged it up to the station concourse and discovered that B had left her ticket on the train. We couldn't get out unless we bought a new ticket. Eventually, the ticket collector was persuaded to let us through and out we went into torrential rain to find a taxi.

81

At the hotel Mrs Fanny, the agency owner, was there to meet us. B had a chance to clean up before we had an 18.00 banquet with the prospective client. A gastronomic challenge for us both, especially B.

Thursday 9/3/06

At 04.00 B was violently sick again. It was clear she must rest, so I met Elliner and Fanny at breakfast and they made arrangements for her to have a late check out at 14.00 and stay in bed while we visited the schools. She would take a taxi direct to the airport at 14.00.
I went off with my luggage with Elliner and Fanny at 09.15. Our first visit was to a kindergarten and primary school. It was very interesting. Children board from 2 years of age. I saw an English class with 3 year-olds. Thence, by car, to see their middle school, a huge campus for 4000 boarding students. I visited classes and met staff. With four executive staff including two Principals we drove off for a massive lunch with many delicacies including roast duck feet. However, most challenging was a dish with slivers of thin slices of some tentacled sea creature, in a sauce so strong that it literally rendered me breathless. The feast over, we drove to the airport to catch the plane to Shenzhen. B arrived safely 20 minutes after us, a great relief to see her, even though she was very shaky. Anna and Mike are moving from Salisbury to Sussex today. It is very unfortunate we can't be there to help them. On the plane, not being disposed to eat yet another meal, I wrote up my diary. We were warned that the temperature in Shenzhen would be 23C, 10C higher than Zhengzhou! A well ordered arrival at Shenzhen with a car waiting. Unfortunately, we were booked (by the agent) into the inaptly named Grand Hotel, a dreadful subterranean room, no windows and very noisy.

Friday 10/03/06

I spent a couple of hours working and then went to meet George, from the agency, in the foyer at 11.30 to go shopping. He told me that the whole firm is wanting to meet us in a restaurant for lunch. They are so kind but all this fibreless food is just too much, I am longing for a salad!
A convivial lunch. I took farewells of all except Elliner who we will see this evening and George who we will meet at 14.30 for another shopping foray. Back to the hotel and then 19.00 we went to meet Ruby, Elliner and George for another banquet which we are paying for this time.

Saturday 11/03/06

Not a good day to make the foot crossing to Hong Kong!! It was teeming with people. We left our hotel at 10.00 and arrived in Hong Kong on the southern side of the border at 13.00 after endless queuing. They are so patient, but frightful queue jumpers! We stopped for a rest and a coffee then caught the train to Tsin Tsi Chiu. Our hotel is wonderful after the Grand in Shenzhen! A fantastic vista across to Hong Kong Island from our room.

Sunday 12/03/06

Today B left for England and I met up with Martin Lemon who was to take over the Salisbury School of English. We embarked on a tour of SSE agents to introduce him and his organisation to them. The tour together ended in Xiajiou on 15th March.

Wednesday 15/3/06

We checked in to a hotel next to Xiajiao office before the meeting. To my relief, Rose whom we have worked with for 3 years led the meeting. I haven't seen her since last year's barn dance in Salisbury when I stood on her foot and near hospitalised her. After a quick change, at 18.35 we met for dinner in the same room and at the same table as we had had the famous snake soup episode on our last visit. No snakes this time but plenty of other exotica, mainly of the marine variety this being a seaside city. Mr Loo, the owner/manager of the Xiajiao agency had insisted that we should have a seaside tour. A car duly turned up and we were whisked off in the dark! It is very kind of them but truly absurd. We couldn't see anything, but we were told that it is possible to see Taiwan from the coast road.
After this meeting Martin returned to Hong Kong and I had decided to spend the last day of my trip visiting a new agent in Chongqing who had asked to meet me.

Thursday 16/3/06

The alarm went off at 05.30, I checked out at 06.00 and took a taxi to the airport. Bizarre breakfast and then embarked at 07.40 for Chongqing with an en route landing at Guilin. At Guilin we were told to leave the aircraft for 20 minutes. The airport toilets were worth a comment. The men's department was heavily scented, not the normal pungency, but joystick coils smoking on the urinals. The hand washing area was communal unisex.
At Chongquin I met Zoe, the manager's PA, who had a car waiting. About 20 minutes to central Chongqing, a modern city of 6 million. Their offices turned out to be on the 5th floor of the 5 star Marriot Hotel. Most imposing. I met the boss, Mr Wang, who was at first very po-faced 30 something year-old. He told me he wanted to book at least 150 places in Weymouth. I was concerned about his ability to get visas, a worry he quickly dismissed. It turned out that he also owned the UK Visa application centre which was in the same building. After a preamble we went for a superb lunch at the Marriot. After lunch we got down to detail. He presented me with a splendid book for Dad on the 3 Gorges Dams. Also crafted wooden chop sticks for me. We finished our meeting at 15.00 when he suggested that we continue with a walk in the city centre and a relaxed conversation. He led us (Zoë & me) up some plain steps to what turned out to be a massage parlour. We entered a dimly lit room with 3 exotic couches complete with pillows and duvets. We took our shoes off and in came 3 young ladies in white tracksuits and the foot massage began. It started at the upper thigh and moved down eventually to the feet, after first bathing them in a bowl of herbal infusion. Mr Wang promptly fell asleep, but my concern about what would happen kept me awake. The whole procedure took 1 ½ hours and ranged from pleasure to pain, (they cracked each toe joint), with tickles in between. We finished in time to get back to the office to collect my bags and take a private driver to the airport. I took the 18.35 flight to Guangzhou, and the day after returned to UK.

Belgium

We had very few Belgian students so it is relatively easy to remember those we had. Apart from one young man who took a very demonstrative shine to Anna, then aged 16, the most memorable was a one-to-one student whom I taught for much of his two week course. Monsieur Le Grand was anything but grand in height. He was portly and had a substantial moustache; he was also big on personality and charm. A dapper dresser who arrived for class each day looking as if he were on his way to a party, he was a very important contact for us to get an entry into the heavy engineering company where he worked as a manager.

On Thursday, the penultimate day of his course, I went through his course appraisal with him. It was very positive apart from "Social Activities" where he had noted that he had not had a chance to use his hiking boots during his stay in Salisbury. He had read that it was a place which offered many opportunities for walking, a pastime of which, he stated, he was very fond. Ever keen to keep a smile on the faces of students I suggested that we take our last day's tuition on the downs and take a long walk. He readily agreed.

On Friday morning Barbro gave us a lift to a spot where the Ox Drove crossed the Salisbury to Shaftesbury road. The Ox Drove is an ancient track once used to drive farm animals to Salisbury. Like most such tracks it follows high ground to avoid the once boggy valleys and the views are quite stunning. The distance to Salisbury was about twenty kilometres. With the wisdom of hindsight this was quite an impractical undertaking! I knew nothing of his physical fitness and did not consider that fondness for walking may not mean being fanatical about it. We took no refreshment with us as I intended to descend into the village of Fovant to take a pub lunch, before resuming with a post prandial stroll the rest of the way.

Monsieur Le Grand duly appeared at the School in walking boots at 09.15 wearing orange and brown check plus-fours and a matching hunting jacket, the whole ensemble topped off with a pert little red cap. Poirot would have approved.

The beginning of the walk from the main road is up a very long, steep track to the trail on the top of the hill. It quickly became apparent that Mr Le Grand was not used to hill walking. I slowed to a sauntering pace attempting to pretend that this was my usual gait and thus not embarrass him. Eventually, we reached the summit by which time my companion's complexion matched his cap and his gasping for breath prevented any attempt at English vocabulary enrichment which might have been part of our perambulatory lesson, for some time.

Once on the more level ground he recovered and we enjoyed the sunshine and the fine views. We had much jovial conversation and the walk, now at a fairly sedentary pace, was most enjoyable for both of us. By quarter past one we had both remarked on how much we were looking forward to refreshment at the pub. However, by this time I realised how much behind schedule we were.

Far away ahead of us, down in the valley I could see the village of Fovant. We had to walk level with the village and then descend by a track to the pub. I began to be increasingly gripped by the terrifying thought that we were not going to get there before pub closing time at two o'clock and in the meantime we would both run out of energy.

Eventually, I found courage to tell my portly companion that we would have to speed up or we might be too late for lunch. This fact invoked horror in him, almost panic.

"It would be the quickest for us to walk direct to the village, the shortest distance is the line which is straight!" he wailed. Now in danger of upsetting this important client through starving him, I reluctantly agreed. I could see the pattern of the fields, some arable, some with cows grazing in them. I knew for certain that the fencing around them would be substantial.

With the thought of missing his lunch driving him, he was quickly through the low hedge and over the harmless sheep fencing which marked the edge of the path. I followed. If Monsieur Le Grand was slow going uphill he was like a sprinter with the slope in his favour. I lumbered behind as he trotted diagonally across the empty field, his red cap bobbing with every jaunty step. We arrived at the far corner and the real challenge faced us. We would have to climb over a barbed wire fence placed on top of the sheep fencing. His enthusiasm was only dulled when his jacket caught on the wire at his first attempt to get astride it. He wrenched free to the accompaniment of a high pitched ripping sound and a fine piece of tweed was left decorating the wire.

I would gladly have been swallowed up by the fine Fovant earth. This was embarrassing to the nth degree. There were two choices, to trek back up the hill and find a more accessible route or to make a thoroughly scientific approach to scaling the barrier before us. The former would probably cause us to miss lunch; the latter would require some agreement between us on a strategy which would cause minimum damage to body and attire.

In the corner of the field the fence was supported by one vertical post which was buttressed by two diagonal supports, each in line with one run of the fence. This I decided was the weak point in our enemy's defence. A preliminary assault showed that the diagonals could be used to climb on to get one foot on to the top of the barbed wire and then all that was necessary was a leap on to the grass beyond. At this point I reminded myself that I was considerably more athletic than Monsieur Le Grand. I decided that he would have to test the theory first as I would need to help him to scale the diagonal. I willingly got on my knees before him so that he could step on to my back, thence to the top of the diagonal, assume a precarious balance on top of the offending wire and finally launch himself to the ground on the far side.

Having descended from the heights, the land we were now on was considerably muddier. I assumed position before him, hands and knees in the mire. It worked! With surprising agility, after almost crushing my ribs and with a temporary totter on the top wire he jumped.

I had noticed that on the other side of the fence there was a trough for the cows to drink, but both the trough and the cows were at sufficient distance from the corner as not to present a danger to interlopers leaping the fence. However, what I had not considered was that since the cows would, quite naturally at times of thirst, all gather round the trough, they would while waiting, defecate with gay abandon.

Monsieur Le Grand landed gymnastically on his feet in a minefield of cow dung. To show solidarity I did the same, but took my aim as carefully as possible. After some brief attempt to clean our boots we resumed our trot and reached the far side of the field where to our relief there was an easily scalable gate. We marched determinedly through a farmyard to the accompaniment of the farm dogs yelping, fortunately they were all in an enclosure, and found ourselves on the main road but a hundred metres from the pub.

As we approached the door of the pub I glanced at my watch and saw that we had five minutes to spare before afternoon closing time. There were two locals sitting at the bar who turned to us when we went in. The usual perfunctory glance given to strangers became a stare. The sight before them was of a mud bespattered pair of tramps. My hands were caked in mud and my light walking trousers were mired from the knees down. My companion was less dramatically marked, but he was contaminated with bucolic compounds which must have already permeated the air of the bar. His torn jacket did nothing to dispel our appearance of men of the road.

I explained our plight to them and suffered the indignity of their amusement while trying to persuade the barmaid that we would be able to afford the fayre on offer.

"The kitchen is closed now love", she told me. Desperation gripped me; I sidled up to the bar and with a muddy hand proffered her a ten pound note.

I whispered, "Could you open it again, all we need is some sandwiches". She took the note and pushed the sandwich menu towards me.

Once having cleaned ourselves such as we could, I borrowed the pub phone and called Barbro to come to pick us up. As the bar was closing we doubled our beer order and awaited our sandwiches. Monsieur Le Grand looked at me over the froth on his pint, his eyes narrowed, is this

his rage building up I wondered? He lowered the glass and I saw that he was grinning, his fine moustache stretching across his face. I grinned, he started to laugh, my pent up anxiety released and I found myself in paroxysms of laughter, as did he. The day was saved! But lost somewhere, probably decorating a hedge, there was a pert little red cap which would not see Belgium again.

Korea

Unfortunately I never had the chance to visit Korea, despite the fact that at one time it was a major adult student market for us. We had a few Korean teenagers groups but the one I remember most vividly was inherited from another school in Salisbury, as they were unable to offer residential accommodation. It is however, a course which we will never forget!

The course itself went well, but one evening there was a major issue at St Mary's residential centre which caused a considerable upset. When the facts had been explained after the event, we were able to establish exactly what had happened.

One afternoon, a car which was being driven by a Korean adult, not a student at the School, stopped outside MacDonald's. For some reason there was an exchange of words between him and one of our Korean teenagers. The latter appears to have used insulting terminology which greatly incensed the driver.

Around eleven in the evening I received a message asking for immediate support for our staff at St Mary's as there was an ongoing "incident". On arrival I was confronted by a crowd of Koreans and their male leader. All the windows overlooking the quadrangle appeared to be open with students of many nationalities peering out watching the events unfold.
I had arrived too late to intervene in a "ritual" punishment of one of the boys by the group leader, which had been viewed by the rest of the student corps and their group leaders and upset many of them.

I was told that the Korean group leader had paraded all his students and then singled out one of their number. This lad had been made to kneel on all fours. The leader had broken a plank from the fence and the boy had been thrashed across the backside with the plank.

This was quite horrifying stuff and I anguished about whether to call the police to arrest the group leader, but thought better of it when I considered the possible diplomatic consequences.

I took the plank from the leader and demanded an explanation. He told me quite coolly that as the boy had insulted an adult in a terrible way he had to be punished. Apparently, the adult Korean had turned up at the residential centre at half past ten demanding retribution for the loss of face he had suffered. The alleged miscreant was identified and the summary punishment had taken place in order to pacify and satisfy the accuser. The leader really could not understand my indignation.

A dramatic example of a culture clash.

We did, however, have a much more pleasant experience with another Korean client. We had had an enquiry about arranging a long term, two-to-one course for two sisters, aged 11 and 13. The parents wanted the girls to improve their English to a level where they could enrol at the Godolphin School. Normally we would not have taken such young students outside of the summer season, but the parents insisted and said that they would arrange accommodation in a rented house and that the children's grandmother would stay at the house to look after them.

The course went well, but it soon became obvious that the grandmother, who did not speak English, was somewhat bored spending so much time alone. She came to the school each day at lunch time to give the girls their home cooked Korean food. Soon, the lady started coming earlier and earlier. She had decided that some of the teaching staff, and in particular Martin Goddard, looked underfed and so she brought food for their lunch too. This was extremely generous and thoughtful of her.

Korean food can be extremely pungent and grandmother's cooking often was. I could tell when grandmother had arrived from the powerful odours wafting up to my office. At first the staff gratefully accepted the free meals, but soon they had had their fill of the strong flavours. Then grandmother turned her attention to me and the office staff, for by this time, teachers had resorted to hiding when she arrived. Now when she came, she requested that I should be summoned. Unless I could find a very good excuse not to, good manners dictated that I should greet her and sample today's cooking. This went on for several weeks until her daughter, the girls' mother came to stay and grandmother turned her attention to feeding her.

Spain

In the early years we had no students from Spain at all and it was not until I travelled to Bilbao in about 1988 that we got any business from that country. In Bilbao I met Txema and his wife. He ran a private school and each summer sent students to England. He sent us a small group, which he accompanied himself, and then our co-operation continued for many years. But he was not an easy man to deal with.

Whenever we were negotiating prices he rejected the idea of a fixed price list and argued forcibly to get the lowest price possible. He would start by saying "But Mi-ike, this is Txema, your best customer, I need a very special price".

Neither was this the only challenge in dealing with him. When a course was underway he would constantly ask for students to be promoted to a higher level. If, on sound educational grounds we refused, he would never give in and loudly pursued the Director of Studies relentlessly until we decided that we would have to buy peace in the School, by giving in.

I cannot remember which year Estrella Osuna first came to us but it must have been in the late eighties. She was one of four remarkable Spanish leaders, all outstanding in different ways. However, what they had in common was dedication to their students and considerable energy.

Estrella brought quite large groups of students and although she sometimes had a university student to help her, she managed the group almost entirely by herself. Though slight of figure and not portraying physical strength, she walked all of her students home each evening after activities, and of course they were in different parts of the City. It was partly my awareness of the effort she had to put into this that made me decide that we needed to offer a free transport scheme to get all students safely home after evening events.

Fina first came to us in 1986. She was an effervescent Catalan group leader with boundless enthusiasm. She had a way of ignoring adversity and finding solutions to whatever problems cropped up. An incredible positive thinker and an excellent group leader who gave me and my staff huge support.

Fina's close friend and colleague in Salisbury was Chus. Despite the fact that Fina was a Catalan nationalist and Chus, who comes from Salamanca, is Spanish through and through, these ladies worked outstandingly well together.

She was another exemplary group leader; firm but fair with the children, with an empathetic understanding of the difficulties of running summer courses.

In the mid nineties a Spanish Army officer, Antonio, attended a course. He returned for several consecutive years bringing with him several of his six children. He recommended the School to the Spanish Officer Training Academy in Zarragoza and thus started a most successful co-operation which lasted for many years.

Chus Calvo

The Academy sent groups of over a hundred officer cadets, together with a commanding officer, to England each summer for a three week course. First we had a large group and then SSE contracted with the Academy to arrange courses for groups of maximum eight cadets to be taught in different schools. It was my responsibility to choose the schools taking part in the project, to brief them on the educational aims of the course and to make all the practical and travel arrangements. Thus I had the pleasure of awarding sub-contracts to other schools which I respected.

A Spanish Army group, with one stowaway! Antonio is on the left. Julian Lewis on the right

The cadets were extremely popular with the schools. Their behaviour was excellent, they studied hard and since they were in the main, a very presentable bunch of men, they added some excitement to the often female dominated classes. (In later years there were actually female officer cadets in the groups too). When arranging accommodation the standard questions from the Accommodation Officer were, "does this student smoke, is he allergic to anything, does he mind pets?" The answer from high command was always that they will not smoke, they will not be allergic and they will like pets.

The commander of the whole group each year was usually a major or a colonel and he stayed in Salisbury. We arranged free private lessons for this officer. Sometimes they brought their families, in which case we gave what perks we could. One of these officers, a major, had just returned from a tough six month tour of peace keeping duty in Bosnia before taking command of the group. He had survived his Balkan experience without a scratch, but in Salisbury he ended up in hospital.

We had arranged a flat for the major and his family. One fine day the family were on the balcony of the flat and the major decided to put up the parasol. He misjudged the weight of the device and dropped it on his foot, spike first. He spent the rest of his time with us with his foot in plaster and hobbling with a crutch. Needless to say, this occasioned some mirth amongst his men.

The Arab World

As I have recounted elsewhere, over the years we had a small number of Arab students, mainly from the Gulf States, who were sponsored by military authorities in their own countries. It was not until quite late on that we established market contacts which provided a regular flow of Arab adult students to the School. The same is true of courses for teenagers. We were lucky enough to have a significant number of extended families which sent brothers, sisters and cousins each summer, but in the last few summers we had some Arab groups. Generally, our experience with Arab students was very positive, and if there were difficulties it was usually because of our lack of familiarity in dealing with students from the Middle East.

There were of course cultural misunderstandings, the most memorable of which led to a failed property purchase. This incident arose when the father of a Saudi student visited the School one Friday afternoon and said that he wanted his son to have private accommodation, he would like to buy a house for him. He asked if I knew of any house for sale and so I took him to visit a new housing estate.

I made an appointment with the sales office of the estate developers and we agreed to meet their salesman at a house which had been the show home on the estate. When we arrived the father was shown round and he seemed quite keen on the house. Then he started to ask questions which floored the bewildered representative. Could he arrange for this wall to be knocked down? Could this room be extended into the garden? And so on. I tried to explain to the father that the house was for sale in its present state and that the buyer would have to make any changes he required. Eventually, he accepted this notion and asked the sales representative how much the house cost. Sixty nine thousand pounds, he was told.

If the poor salesman was nonplussed now, it soon got worse for him.

"I give you the money in cash tomorrow," said the father.

"But, but you have to have a solicitor to make the arrangements."

One can understand the father's difficulty in understanding why this man would not just take his cash for the house. I took over and tried to explain the need for conveyancing. Eventually, the father accepted this curious English concept and asked me to arrange for a solicitor immediately.

I was lucky enough to catch my solicitor before he disappeared for the weekend and he kindly agreed to meet us. So, I drove off with father and son to the lawyer's office. The solicitor gave a long-winded explanation of the formalities, so long-winded that I could see the prospective buyer's enthusiasm visibly waning. When we were once more back at the School the father said to me, "Mr Mike, why I have to pay this lawyer, the price is sixty nine thousand pounds, this lawyer should be included in the price, no extras."

I feebly tried to defend the concept, but clearly I did not succeed. On Monday, the son came to school and asked for us to arrange family accommodation for him.

In our time at SSE we had the privilege of meeting some remarkably generous people. One of them was Salah, a Saudi businessman. He had booked an eight week course for his four children and his wife, and said that from time to time he too would also like to attend classes. The biggest challenge was that he wished to rent a large house in the centre of the City with no expense spared. Barbro was up to the challenge and booked a fine four double bedroomed period house which had recently been refurbished. Another of Salah's requests was that there should be high speed broadband at the house. Unfortunately, there was not, so he asked for this facility to be installed, for which he would pay. This was arranged.

The family duly arrived and the mother and four daughters started their courses. All seemed well with the arrangements apart from a problem with the internet which prevented Salah's computer from connecting. We sent our resident nerd, our nephew Johan, to investigate. He managed to set up Salah's laptop and get everything working well, for which our guest was extremely grateful. After several days we found out why.

Salah usually got to school late, sometime after his family had appeared for their lessons. When he came in he often sat in the School office, opposite Mike Thatcher on reception, and had a chat. Gradually, Mike was able to find out why he was delayed each morning.
Salah was a "market maker". Early each morning when the Saudi stock market opened, he would choose stocks to invest in. He was so well known that others followed his buying patterns. This drove up prices to a point where the sensible investors, Salah included, would sell.

Some mornings he would report to Mike the amount he had earned that day, he seldom lost, but when he did he was philosophical about it. In short, he was a very wealthy man. He had a considerable property portfolio, a farm and a holiday house with servants in Egypt.

After two weeks he asked if his nephews could also enrol with the school. Presumably, they had been studying at another school for there was no requirement for them to get visas. They turned up and joined the family at the house.

One day, while sitting in front of Mike's desk, he must have noticed Mike's worn shoes. "How many pairs of shoes do you have Mike?" he asked.

Mike told him that he had but a few. This shocked Salah who immediately asked Mike's shoe size. Next day he arrived with a new pair of fine leather shoes for Mike.

By way of thanks to Johan, for setting up his computer, he gave him cash to pay the course fee for an introductory course in stock broking! For our part he offered Barbro and me the use of his house in Egypt and promised a chauffeur and house staff.

It was clear that some rich Arabs were not used to taking no for an answer. The Friday, before our busiest week of the summer one year, the parent of children who had been at the School in past years, telephoned to say that his sons were coming on Monday. Barbro had no suitable accommodation left and the Monday classes were full, so she tried to tell the father that we could not take the children. The more she said that we could not take them, the more determined the father became. Barbro got the last word and firmly refused to take the students. On Monday they turned up for school bearing gifts from the parents!

Central and South America

In the late nineties we were fortunate enough to obtain the services of Diana Marshall to promote SSE in parts of the world where we had no or little market. Her sales trips on our behalf to South America were very successful and from having no students at all from that continent we soon had groups from Brazil, Chile, Argentina and Mexico.

Diana and Elizabeth

Most of these students came during their summer holidays. This meant that we found ourselves running a summer school in January and February! This was hugely beneficial all-round. We were able to keep our host families happy; our teachers occupied and of course provide a significant boost to our cash flow at a difficult time of the year. In addition to this, it was really fun to lighten up the winter darkness with lots of cheerful and lively students.

The biggest contingent was always from Brazil and they were usually led by the indomitable, ebullient Elizabeth Schelb. She was a terrific leader who supported her students in every way and was always helpful and positive to the School management. Some of her students could be a little difficult, few were used to looking after themselves, most had maids in Brazil, but she was always like a mother hen with time for everybody.

That is not to say that all her students were angels. One day she got a report that a student had been seen with a gun. She identified the student and informed me. We discovered that the boy had managed to buy a ball bearing firing pistol from a dubious source in Salisbury. He had intended to smuggle it back to Brazil. With visions of what might have happened at security control at the airport we both very quickly got the weapon destroyed!

Our experience with Argentina was also very positive. The group leaders were very good and the children were well motivated. However, the owner of the agency, P.C., could be a challenge. Our agreement with her was that she would have exclusivity for students from Argentina. We intended this to mean that hers was the only agency which could send students to our school.

One day an Argentinean adult walked into the School. She was working locally and wanted some English lessons. In all innocence I informed the agent that since this lady had come directly to us, I did not consider that we could refuse her having lessons. The effect of this message was incendiary. P was incandescent and demanded that we should refuse to take the student. Diana had to mediate and several phone calls later managed to calm the fiery P. We agreed to pay commission on the lady's course fees.

Some Chilean leaders were renowned for disloyalty to their course organisers. The leaders, teachers from the schools where the students studied in their own country, usually asked for a meeting with me on the first day of their courses. At these meetings they would inevitably tell me that next year they could bring a much larger group if I agreed to work directly with them and bypass the agent. Needless to say I never accepted their offers, but it was often awkward, with them badgering me for the whole period of the course.

The enduring memory of the January "Summer School" was the end of course parties. They were loud, colourful and extremely lively. Everyone danced, sang and contributed to the wonderful atmosphere. The sight of a hundred South American children doing English barn dancing under the competent direction of our resident showman, Ian Puffett, was unforgettable.

Angola

We were very surprised to get business from Africa. The first student was a bank manager from Togo, then through amateur radio friends an oil company executive from Guinea Bissau. However, by far the biggest client was Angolan Oil. We had a series of one-to-one students from this company and then, while we were at Salt Lane, we won a contract for a group of coastguards.

This group arrived on a Sunday in the second week of January. I met them from the train and was quite alarmed to see that they had no winter clothes at all. In fact they were wearing short sleeve shirts and light trousers. They had quite literally been lifted out of an African summer and into a cold European winter. The fact that each of them had luggage which comprised one briefcase, betrayed the fact that they did not have coats. The cold was a real and unpleasant novelty for them. After they were dispersed to their host families we started getting phone calls from the families who were worried about the young men's lack of winter wear.

The next morning the students were brought to school by their host families and thus had no exposure to the winter weather. However at lunch time they went off to explore the City. After a while we received a phone call from a shop keeper in town to say that one of the students was in his shop in a distressed state. The young man had collapsed outside of the shop, suffering from hypothermia. Action was called for. We made sure that the students were taken home after school and informed the host families that we would take them shopping on Tuesday, market day.

I took the group around the market stalls buying heavy jackets, scarves, hats and gloves. By midday they were all kitted out with winter wear. At first they found it difficult to get used to the clothes, but there was no doubting the necessity for it. One enduring picture I have in my mind is that of one of the group, so intrigued by and proud of his gloves, wore them continuously, even in lessons!

When the students left in the autumn, they went to Norway. The Norwegian government, as part of their foreign aid programme, had given a fisheries protection vessel to Angola. Our job was to bring the students' level of English up to a point where they could travel to Norway and undertake training, in English, to crew the vessel. This was a very interesting and rewarding project. The students were very sociable and since they were with us during the summer, they were able to enjoy a very busy activities programme. However, there was something of a culture clash when they attended the fancy dress party. They came dressed as a group of disabled beggars.

Japan

I have described elsewhere how the School first entered the Japanese market. We were indeed lucky and developed good links with a number of individuals in Japan who provided us with enrolments of university students and groups of teenagers. Indeed, such was the popularity of Salisbury that we did not actually make a sales trip to Japan until the year 2000.

Our prime contact for students was Bunka University, (Bunka means culture). Not only was the university huge but its educational foundation owned a prestigious private school for girls, Sugunami High School. The latter school sent large groups of girls to us twice a year, in March and August. The School was very formal, in the first years of our co-operation the girls had to wear their uniforms in Salisbury and on excursions. The teacher and tour guides' uniform was a black suit.

Through the years the formality of dress, student behaviour and indeed personal relations between staff, diminished. But in the early years it was quite normal for the Japanese staff to appear at the New Forest barbecue (a most informal event!), in their dark suits, ties and city shoes. On one occasion there was a plague of flying ants. These creatures, for some reason appeared to be attracted by black, it was as much as Louis Snook (who was helping at the barbecues), and I could do to keep straight faces as our Japanese colleagues fled before the swarms.

Seldom, if ever, had we and our staff been photographed so much as we were at the farewell parties. One could see students in little gaggles daring each other to come forward and ask, "Can I take a picture with you?"

The Japanese staff also took photos almost continuously, often for promotional purposes for the next year's course.

The certificate award ceremony took place at the end of course

Their photography went to an extreme when one of the girls ended up in hospital. One of our evening activities in the early days was a roller skate disco. One of the girls slipped up and, we learnt later, broke her coccyx. The event was held just across the road from the local hospital, then in Fisherton Street, so rather than ring for an ambulance, two staff carried the girl to the Accident and Emergency department. This journey was photographed and video filmed as was the subsequent visit to the X-ray department. All the while the poor girl was in agony.

And so in 2000, Barbro and I accepted the longstanding and often repeated invitation to visit our friend Yoshi Tomuro in Tokyo. It was an unforgettable journey, part business part pleasure. Yoshi arranged visits to the University for us to meet colleagues who had been in Salisbury and then, subsequently, to attend an informal get together at a restaurant. On the latter occasion much saki flowed and our hosts were most keen for me to drink as much of it as possible. However, I did not find it to be particularly strong and they were quite confounded that I did not fall flat on my face. Then, one of their number hit on another test for me, he asked me if I had ever eaten puffer fish. I had not but I was aware that the liver of this fish is deadly poison and that eating such fish was a form of Russian roulette which depended on the skill of the chef to completely remove the toxins.

Puffer fish was ordered. When it arrived, the news of the foreigner's possible impending demise had reached all the diners in the restaurant. People were standing on seats to watch as I tucked into the little fish. I could not avoid being theatrical and feigning fear and pretending to collapse, but it won a good round of applause.

As part of our induction into Japanese culture, Yoshi had arranged for us to go a matinee performance of kabuki. I am not sure what we expected. From the description given to us, it was some form of traditional dramatic opera and that was not far wrong. Yoshi disappeared saying that he had some business to attend to, and that in two hours time one of his colleagues, Mr Ito, and his wife would come to take our seats when we left. At that time he would be waiting for us outside the theatre. We noticed that many of the women audience were dressed in traditional Japanese kimonos. This was quite confusing as often the actors appeared from behind us and entered the stage from the passages between the seats. We were not sure who were actors and who were audience. The first hour was interesting indeed, but we gradually tired of watching the performance as we just could not understand the interminable plot. Clearly, kabuki watchers must have great stamina. After two hours we were glad to make our escape.

The main event of our formal programme was a visit to Suginami High School. And formal it was. Barbro and I turned out in our most conservative attire and mounted the steps to the huge school. At the top of the steps we were received by the official welcoming delegation of school notables. On being ushered into an entrance hall almost the size of our school we were requested to leave our shoes on the racks set up for this purpose. On top of the racks were soft slippers which were to be worn by visitors. One look warned me of impending embarrassment. My shoes are size 46, a size unknown in Japan. I went along the row and selected the largest pair of slippers. My heels hung over the back of the footware and the only way I could locomote without losing them was to slide my feet along the stone floors. It was thus in such a fashion that I glided around the school visiting various classrooms and facilities. After watching an alarmingly violent display by fourteen year old girls of some form of martial arts, I was informed that the students were assembling to hear my speech. Speech! No one had told me that a speech was expected. I racked my brain thinking of the fine moral tales expounded on every speech day I had dozed through in England, and did not come up with any ideas.

We entered the auditorium through a stage door and I slid my way across to the lectern. Instantaneous deafening applause broke out as I took my place with Barbro beside me. I looked at the sea of white faces framed with a standard school cut of black hair. There were hundreds of them all standing in perfectly straight rows absolutely accurately, equally spaced. The clapping subsided as the Principal waved a sign which clearly denoted that that was enough for the moment.

To this day I do not remember which story I told them, was it of Robert the Bruce and the spider or Florence Nightingale? Anyway, in best Victorian style I told them an ethical tale. At the end of the speech girls appeared with heaps of flowers and the clapping reached another crescendo. We were whisked from the auditorium, or in my case shuffled from the hall, to the Principal's private dining room where we had an exquisite Japanese sushi meal presented in lacquer boxes. When asked if we had enjoyed the thick slice of raw tuna both Barbro and I said how delicious it was. In truth, while we had dealt with the other fishy items with some relish, the raw tuna was a challenge. A mistake! The Principal spoke to his deputy who disappeared in the direction of the kitchen. A few moments later two even thicker raw tuna slices were delivered to us.

The reception we received and the generous hospitality we enjoyed at the School and at the University were exceptional and we were truly grateful for such an experience.

The executive staff at Suginami high school.
Note my undersized slippers!

Chapter 9   People

Through the years our existence has been enriched by meeting or employing many wonderful people and a good few characters of note. Here is a selection of people who have touched our lives.

Yoshi Tomuro

In the spring of 1990 we received a request from a Japanese educational foundation, Bunka, for a delegation to visit our school with a view to placing teenage students with us. We had had very little experience of Japanese students and none at all of Japanese teenagers. Late one afternoon in May, a coach pulled up outside the School and the delegation disembarked and came in. The delegation comprised three teachers and two representatives of the Foundation's travel service, one of whom, the manager, was Yoshi Tomuro. The meeting was cordial though we were very nervous as we really wanted to get the business and we found it very difficult to interpret the reactions of the group to the answers we provided to their numerous questions. We learnt later that we were the sixth school they had visited that day and that they had made up their minds about awarding the contract to another school and only came to see us out of politeness. We must have made a good impression, as they changed their minds.

Through the years Bunka gave us a huge amount of business. We had large groups of teenagers and later substantial groups of university students. Yoshi accompanied most of the groups and we got to know him very well indeed. Despite the vast cultural divide between us we had shared values and sense of humour. In a few business relationships there is a transition between being commercial partners and being real friends. The exact boundary between the two is indefinable and not to be identified, but when you look forward to spending time with a client and have no particular commercial motive, the boundary has been crossed.

During each course, Yoshi took us out for a meal, together with his senior colleagues, at an expensive restaurant. On one Thursday evening we had chosen to dine at the Rose and Crown hotel. We duly arrived and Yoshi marched up to the head waiter to announce that he had a booking for six.

"What was the name sir?"

"Tomuro of Bunka"

"I am sorry sir; we do not have a booking in that name"

"But I telephoned this morning!"

The waiter flicked through the bookings. "Ah, yes sir, we do have a booking for you for tomorrow."

"But I booked for today?"

The waiter went to consult a colleague. "My colleague took the booking and he says that you booked for Bunka for tomorrow."

"What I said was not for tomorrow but for Tomuro!"

We got our table!

Yoshi loved golf and we knew that if he told us that he was going to the golf course, then he was totally confident that all was going well with the course and he could relax. He bought a set of clubs which he stored at the School and used during his visits. We learnt that at the local golf course he was known as the "pirate". Apparently, because of his stature, his occasional golfing partners had no hesitation to place bets on matches with him. He always took them by surprise and regularly won enough to pay his day fees.

One day, tired of walking to visit host families and off site events, he arrived at school with a very smart new bicycle. He asked us to store it between courses so that it could be used by his staff as required. It became the "Bunka Bike" and as far as I know it is still in the cellar of the School building and indeed, his abandoned golf clubs are still in the attic.

Tom Burke

Tom was a retired Irish railway linesman who wandered into the School one afternoon and asked if we needed a part time gardener. We agreed to employ him for one day a week and occasionally extra days as required. He was an incredibly hard worker who, despite his age, could dig all day and still seem fresh when he went home. He was with us from 1990 until he left very suddenly in 2003. In the early years of his time with us I employed him to do additional work at weekends helping me to landscape the garden. I was doing heavy block work one Saturday when my father came to visit. Tom saw him looking at me, but did not realise that he was my father. He whispered to Dad, "That's the boss, he's a real grafter!" Praise indeed from someone with his work ethic. He always came to work at 07.45 and liked a quick chat before he started. One day he regaled Barbro and me about difficulties he had had at the weekend with his own garden.

"Oi digs down and finds a bat." he told us. "Ee were so heavy I got the neighbour to help."

What manner of bat might this be we wondered. We asked him to explain. "Ee were six foot." He said, irritated that we did not grasp what he meant. The mystery deepened, but we had a school to open for the day and so did not pursue the matter, however, we were intrigued and so at the end of the day I gingerly questioned him again. I asked him what he had done with the "bat".
"Oi giv it ta the farmer for waterin' the cows."

The penny dropped, the "bat" was a "bath" disguised by Irish brogue.

There was a sinister side to Tom. He jealously guarded his rights as gardener and made it plain to new employees that the garden was his territory. A newly employed caretaker came to me to complain that Tom had greeted him by grabbing his genitalia hard and threatening worse to come if he dared to infringe Tom's territory. Towards the end of his employment he also started make unwelcome advances to some female employees.

I was considering his future and wrestling with the prospect of finding a new gardener when I met him one day at the front door, on his way out. He looked at me and said, "Boss, oi ain't working 'ere no more."

"Why not Tom?" I asked.

"Oi has mates as gets £6 an hour for this work. I am underpaid."

"But Tom you get £42 a day for working 6 hours."

"That's what I means! I'm goin'."

And that was the last we ever saw of him.

Louis Snook

Louis in action

Several of our host families found their way into employment with the School. Louis and his wife Amarylis, were exceptionally popular with students, several of whom returned year after year, insisting that they should stay with the couple. On 19th May 1989 I interviewed Louis for a job as a minibus driver, he was then in his late sixties. I gave him the job and never regretted it. He was an exceptionally loyal and reliable colleague who became a friend.

Louis' duties included being responsible for the summer Tuesday evening New Forest barbecues. He left Salisbury an hour before the students departed by coach, his minibus loaded with charcoal, lighters, sports equipment and the requisite number of sausages and burgers. His job was to get the fires going in readiness for the hordes descending on the forest.

 And hordes they were, sometimes as many as six fifty-seater coaches disgorged students when they arrived at about eight o'clock. Throughout the time he did this job I drove to the Forest to assist him, but by the time I got there he had the hearths blazing and the volley ball nets up. We then spent a frantic two hours dispensing burgers and sausages to a hungry clientele. Twenty minutes before the students re-embarked to return to the City, he would drive off ahead of them so that he had time to get to the School, unload the sports kit and surplus charcoal, and then be at the coach park to meet the coaches as they came in, to assist the other waiting minibuses in taking children home to their host families.

Sometimes Louis' culinary skills were questioned by group leaders, but never by students. The barbecues were always very popular. They were also sometimes fraught with logistical problems. On several occasions, when Louis arrived at the barbecue site, which we had pre-booked, he found that the site was partially occupied by tourists who had decided to have an informal barbecue. They could not use the hearth as it was locked and Louis had the key, but they often had portable barbecues. Since we needed every available seat for our event we had to politely ask for them to leave. Some did not believe us when we told them that 300 children would be arriving shortly and their peaceful dinner would be somewhat disturbed. In these cases it took the actual arrival of the group to move them.

Towards the end of Louis' time with us, before he moved to Yorkshire, we experienced another kind of inconvenience brought on us by the permanent inhabitants of the forest. Every time I met Louis after the event, we both broke into uncontrolled laughter as soon as it was mentioned. When I arrived at the site, Louis was putting up the volley ball nets but he had not lit the hearth. I asked him what the problem was and he pointed to the area around the big metal barbecue. Clearly, a herd of ponies had spent the day by the hearth. The ground around the cook's side was completely covered with horse dung. We hunted around to try to find some appliance to scoop up the mess but nothing we had brought with us would do the job and the coaches were just half an hour away. Then Louis had an idea, we could use inverted frisbees! We spent twenty minutes feverishly digging and scraping until it was possible to approach the hearth without being ankle deep in manure. As we were doing the job, Louis asked if this shouldn't be in his job description, we looked at each other and just broke down with laughter, the tears running down our cheeks. A wonderful man, whom I am honoured to have worked with.

Edgar

Some things are taken for granted until they are no more. And such was the case of Edgar's bakery. On the corner of Fowlers Road, which led up to the School and Milford Hill, Edgar and his wife had a bakery shop. He was German and she English. Everything they sold was baked on the premises. Their filled bread rolls were the staple lunch time fayre of teachers and students alike. But it was not only the rolls which attracted us, their cakes and pastries were equally popular. The biggest treat of all was when strawberries were in season, many a strawberry tart found its way up the hill to number 36.

This was a real "old fashioned" shop with personal service and oven fresh produce. It was a tragedy therefore when their landlord increased the rent to such an extreme that they had to close. Edgar was forced to seek employment in an industrial bakery and his wife in a supermarket. They were severely missed.

Fred Croft

This is a man who actually never had anything to do with the School, but almost did. He was one of the small group of immediate post war EFL entrepreneurs. When we lived in Whiteparish our next door neighbours were an English and Dutch couple. The English lady introduced me to her father, Fred Croft, at the Whiteparish carnival in 1990. He was already in his late seventies but still ran an EFL school in Romsey.

Fred's story was a remarkable one. He told me that when he came out of the army in 1946 he had no job and only sixpence in his pocket. He was sitting on a bench in Green Park wondering what to do with his life when he heard a group of foreign children trying to communicate with each other in English. That gave him the idea of starting a language school.

As far as I know, Fred had no qualifications whatever, but he had drive and business acumen. Soon he was running a coaching business bringing groups of school children to England for short courses. Somehow he established contacts with prestigious organisations in various countries. He knew President Tito of Yugoslavia and he had close contacts with Opus Deo in Spain. For a time he was the biggest operator in the Yugoslav language market. Eventually, he started a school in Romsey in a disused primary school. When I met him he was still running the school and bringing coach loads of French children to Romsey for short courses.

After our chance meeting he invited me to visit his school and later to have dinner at his home. There he proposed that I should take over his business and amalgamate it with mine. He entreated me in his broad Yorkshire accent, "There's good money in it lad, I make a thousand pounds a coach load and bring in five or six a month."

It very nearly happened. I would like to have brought his school up to the standards we aspired to, and the cash flow was strong. The deal fell at the last hurdle when we were finalising the financial terms of the contract.

Blind students

We were always hungry for business and prepared to adapt to whatever market demand we could identify. Thus it was that over the years we accepted several blind students. The potential problems were formidable. They had to find their way to and from and around the school and to manage in the classroom without taking an undue amount of teacher time and thus annoying other students. Only once we regretted taking a student. One young woman, used to being attended to day and night at home, had to be bathed by the host mother and required constant help. However, two young men were completely different.

M. was a Jordanian student who had been blind from birth. He had succeeded in getting a degree in his own country and now wanted to study for a Phd in the UK. He was remarkably confident. After a few practices he learnt his way to and from school and although he was studying in a group of sighted people he managed his studies efficiently and made few extra demands on the teacher. When he left us he moved to Liverpool to study at the university.

Peter, a young blind adult from an eastern European country was alarmingly self-sufficient. Peter was walked to school on his first morning by his host family. After that, he declared that he would be able to find his own way home and then back to school the next day. With some reluctance we gave in to his insistence that he should walk home alone after his first school day. We sent a member of staff to "shadow" him from a distance, just to make sure that he did indeed get home safely. The teacher came back and related that Peter had stormed off at high speed and though he had encountered some hard objects such as lamp posts, he had navigated successfully with his white stick and had got home safely.

Next day, Peter came to school with a bump on his head, his only visible injury, and remembering the geography of the school from the previous day, found the common room and later his classroom. Needless to say, Peter's remarkable courage and determination made him very popular with teachers and students alike.

He came for several successive years. At first, he always returned to the same host family, though their patience was often tried by the fact that he did not bother to wear clothes in the house. One day the host mother rang Barbro to ask if we could persuade him to dress when he was at home. She related that she had been having a nap on the sofa when she heard a noise, opened her eyes and saw Peter's bare backside descending towards her, he unaware that she was on the sofa.

As the years passed it became clear that Peter's increasing alcohol consumption was affecting his behaviour. He became very unpredictable and his crowning achievement was to clamber through the window of his bedroom and on to the roof. This would not have been so bad if the roof had been flat, but his bedroom window was in a roof sloping at around 45 degrees. His naked form was spotted by a passer-by. He was clinging on to the window sill with his feet perilously close to the guttering and the edge of the roof. He hung on long enough for the fire brigade to get him down safely.

Sir Edward Heath

In the late 1990's we won a contract to run summer courses for members of the Swedish Parliament. These courses were extremely challenging from an organisational and teaching point of view. In addition to specialised language input, the course programme comprised visits from outside speakers and semi-official visits to local government offices. The fact that we retained the contract for five years and indeed widened it to include some Norwegian and Icelandic members of parliament, bears testimony to our success and the skill of the teaching staff.

I was always uneasy about appointing outside speakers for any course as one had a sense of losing control of the quality of a course when bringing in a new untried speaker for the first time. This was not just true for the parliamentary courses but also for other specialised group courses of which we had many. Several times experts in specialised fields such as timber or steel production, turned out to be poor speakers. Thus it was that I took no chances with the parliamentary courses. Our local MP, Robert Key, was a great supporter of the School and an excellent speaker who helped us on many occasions. Paul Sample, a local politician, was also very reliable. However, on one occasion I was able to enlist the services of Sir Edward Heath, who lived in Salisbury, to speak on a parliamentary course. He was excellent and the course participants were enthralled to hear him recounting his experiences in politics from Konrad Adenauer to Margaret Thatcher. He elected to speak in the School garden and we sat in a large circle with him on one side.

Sir Edward did not brook any interruptions. The unflappable Martin Goddard, a most conscientious and reliable man, had been teaching a one-to-one student, an executive from Saab. They decided to take a break from the classroom and stroll on the School terrace continuing chatting.

"I don't talk when I am interrupted," shouted Sir Edward at the distant figures. Martin made a diplomatic retreat.

Sir Edward was much taken by this band of disciples sitting around him and asked what they were doing in the evening, saying that he would be pleased to show them round his house.

The fact was that we had arranged a drinks party for the parliamentarians and some local politicians and businessmen. This was very embarrassing as the course participants clearly preferred the opportunity to visit the grand house in the Cathedral Close to attending the drinks party.

The uneasy compromise reached was that the course members would spend a short while at the party and then in all haste, dash off to the Cathedral Close. Poor Barbro had the job of entertaining the local potentates alone while I went off to accompany the group and show them the way.

The visit to the house was fascinating. Sir Edward was our guide and after a glass of sherry he showed us the various rooms, his music room, his trophy room and so on. One of the Swedes picked up a Chinese vase which was on display in the trophy room and asked how old it was. "Be careful dear chap, that is a Ming Dynasty vase given to me by Mao Zedong."

Another asked him if there was an association of past Prime Ministers. "What on earth would I want to meet that lot for," was the answer.

Fina Coll

Fina first started bringing groups to Salisbury in 1986. Suffice it to say, she was one of the first of our loyal and very effective Spanish group leaders. But to call her Spanish would not meet with her approval. She was from a village outside Barcelona and was an ardent Catalonian nationalist.

Fina had a small private school in her village, which we once had the pleasure of visiting. Each year she recruited a number of her students to bring to Salisbury. Fina chose the students she would accept to take, not on academic ability necessarily, but on the basis of how they might behave away from home. Her standards were high and she would not compromise them. She was a remarkably well organised lady; the pre-course administration was always immaculate.

Physically, Fina was short, in character she was huge. Her energy was prodigious and her enthusiasm infectious. She was strict with her charges, but always fair. From the school's point of view she was an ideal client, all the more so because, since she ran her own school, she understood our difficulties, be they concerned with welfare or academic issues.

Fina was an accomplished mountain walker and regularly went on very long walks in the mountainous terrain around her village. She really was very fit. Thus it came as a great shock, to receive a phone call in September 2007, to hear that she had been found dead in her house, a victim of a heart attack. A real tragedy for her, her family, her students and for her friends, among whom, we were proud to be numbered.

Nick McIver

Nick was quite simply one of the most talented men I have ever had the pleasure of working with. In the early days his talent as an entertainer found expression in our social programme and was a key part of it. As a teacher trainer he was peerless. The quality of his work was held in the highest regard by our clients. However, as the School grew, Nick demonstrated his skill as Director of Studies. Thus it was a disaster for him personally, and a great loss for the School, when the academic requirements for an appointment as Director of Studies, as required by the British Council, were changed in the early nineties and I had to give him notice. This was a dark time for him, but I was soon able to employ him again when it became apparent that our success in the teenage market necessitated the appointment of a Summer Course Director. It was in this role that Nick continued to serve loyally until 2006.

After the School had been sold, Nick increased his commitment to text book writing for Macmillan's publishers. We were all shocked and greatly saddened when Nick died of a heart attack in spring 2011.

Paula Paris and Michel

Paula was a senior judge in France, her area of specialisation was criminal law. I do not know how she found us but we were lucky she did, for she became a good friend and introduced us to some really interesting characters. Paula first came in 1981 and returned to the School year after year, usually in September. At various times we had the pleasure of having some of her friends at the School too. She lived in St Brieuc in Brittany and we visited her there with our children. While we were there we were entertained one evening by Michel, his wife, and their son Antoine.

Michel's wife was an artist and her specialisation, and it was very specialist, was decorating pianos and harpsichords with paintings of a religious nature, angels, cherubs and so on. But she did it very much tongue in cheek. If her paintings were inspected closely, one could see that the faces of the figures were all of her family and friends. Thus one angel was Michel, one cherub Antoine and so on. It was really very clever.

At dinner we heard of some of Michel's exploits. He was a doctor practising in Paris. He had recently been promoted and told us of the day when he had had his interview for the new job. He had left things a bit late when he rushed out of his Paris flat. He ran to his Citroen 2CV and put the key into the lock. It would not turn. He twisted it, turned it and tried every way to get into the car. Desperate, he ran back into the flat and came out with a kitchen knife. He cut through the canvas top of the car and squeezed in through the gap. On putting the key into the ignition he found that it would not turn. Exasperated he sat back in the seat. He glanced in the mirror and saw, two cars back, an identical Citroen 2CV, his car!

When Antoine attended a teenagers' course at SSE, Michel came to collect him on the last day to go on a tour of England. Michel had a complete lack of trust of English food and his Citroen was loaded with food from home, including a supply of baguettes and a crate of wine. They set off on their journey and it was not until later that we heard how his last bottle of wine had been used. Michel smoked a pipe and it was while they were in the north of England that, while driving, he took a rest from puffing and put his lighted pipe on to the dashboard, among maps and papers. The breeze through the primitive air intake did the rest. The papers caught fire. They skidded to a halt.

Fortunately, Antoine was a resourceful boy and saw that the only fluid they had which could douse the flames was the very last, very best, bottle of French wine. He grabbed a corkscrew, opened it and poured the wine over the blaze and put the fire out. The incandescence in the car now was from Michel. He was absolutely furious with Antoine for ruining a bottle of fine wine.

Veronica Dimeo

For a period of over 20 years we had a school cleaner called Veronica. The length of her period of employment bears testimony to how well she did her job and how fond we were of her. Her mother brought her into the School at Rollestone Street one afternoon in 1983 after we had advertised the job of cleaner. This was after we had been forced to sack our first cleaner whom we had nicknamed Flash. The latter lady was vastly overweight and the speed and thoroughness of her cleaning were in inverse proportion to her mass. In fact she was our second cleaner as previously Barbro had done the cleaning.

Veronica was a shy sixteen year-old, but eager to learn and please. We soon became aware that she was one of a family of Jehovah's Witnesses. This was never a problem for us, for although she was strictly religious she satisfied the requirement for evangelism by patrolling the town, canvassing for potential converts, in the mornings. She worked for us in the late afternoon and early evening and we trusted her with the keys and the code to the security system.

She had the secret of being totally unobtrusive and discreet. One was seldom aware of her presence in the building. Yet, she did her job to Barbro's satisfaction, no small order!

Bert Hopkins

Several companies tendered for the work to build the extension to Fowlers Road. The company we chose was not the cheapest but they were highly recommended by our architects. The job of extending the building was made difficult because of severe restrictions placed on us by the Council since the building is in a conservation area. Bricks had to be specially designed and made to match the original Victorian ones, windows had to conform to an exact specification to match the old part of the building, yet they had to be fire proof and double glazed. The whole job was seriously compromised when it was discovered that the consultant employed by the City planning department had made a mistake when making a test excavation to determine how deep the solid chalk strata was. Eventually the foundations had to be two metres deeper than expected. Further, when the free standing garage was demolished it was discovered that underneath it there was a reinforced concrete bomb shelter.

We awarded the contract to Hopkins Builders. The owner was a diminutive character called Bert Hopkins. When I first met him and shook hands with him, I immediately realised that something was amiss. He had but three fingers on his right hand. I never dared to ask how he lost the other two and the handicap never affected his work. Bert's management style was totally hands on. Anything his men could do he could and did do too. He demonstrated graphically that a person does not have to be physically large to manage a team of men. He had their total respect and his experience was clearly much relied on.

Bert was of the old school, problems are there to be overcome. He always led from the front. This was demonstrated in a most extraordinary way when the time came to lift a substantial reinforced steel girder from street level, through a first floor window and into the building. His colleagues were standing around looking at the girder and up at the open window frame, the window itself having been removed. There was much scratching of heads and mutterings about health and safety.

Bert had heard enough. He stood on the bottom rung of the ladder and instructed the men to lift the girder up vertically and to place it on his back. By this time, Barbro and several others of us were at the front of the building to watch the spectacle. Bert had the girder strapped to his back and then slowly, step by step he mounted the ladder with men pushing the metal from below. When he had reached the half way point, several of his men were able to reach out of the window and grab the top of the girder and begin to pull the whole thing up his back and into the room. Bert climbed down the ladder and calmly went up stairs to help the men.

Needless to say Hopkins Builders made an excellent job of the extension.

Teachers

As I have mentioned elsewhere, Salisbury is very much off the beaten EFL track, and was even more so when we started the school. Thus we were pleased and surprised to find so many talented teachers on our doorstep. To my eternal regret, we were never able to employ all the ones we would have liked to, on a permanent contract basis. The other fact of life which is very much to be regretted is that the EFL profession is poorly paid, and while we were as generous as we could afford to be, most teachers did not earn what their talents deserved.

Many hundreds of teachers have worked at the School through the years. I have mentioned some in this book. It would be invidious to single out any particular teacher for praise; suffice it to say that they were all aware that we had to aim high in quality. Everyone recognised that Salisbury was not one of the EFL honey pots and the only way we could attract students was to build a sound and respected reputation in all the school's activities. I would like to pay tribute to one teacher who, sadly, succumbed to cancer. Simon Howarth was a local district councillor as well as a teacher and he always did a sterling job for us on the numerous occasions when we had groups of foreign local government officers studying at the school.

Many of our most loyal and longstanding teachers are shown in the group photograph on the next page. There are so many more that I would like to include if space allowed. One I must mention is Pamela White, a hugely talented teacher and linguist. She seemed to know a lot or a little of many languages and her language learning had given her the talent of being able to empathise with our foreign learners of English. And then there were the Irish! One summer we had so many Irish seasonal employees, led by the indomitable Joe Quinn, (one of several teachers who married colleagues at the school), that a wag christened the School the "Salisbury school of Irish".

Julian Lewis

One of their number, Dermot O'Sullivan, gave a very nervous time to an examiner from the Royal Society of Arts. Dermot used one of his School classes for his obligatory demonstration lesson as part of his Diploma in EFL examination. He hit on the idea of doing an exercise in question forming by getting his students to make up questions about what was in a brown paper parcel on his desk. To add drama to the exercise he put a loudly ticking alarm clock inside the parcel. The examiner, confronted by this wildly gesticulating Northern Irish teacher, in the middle of a period of intense IRA activity in the UK with a ticking parcel on his desk, looked decidedly pale when he emerged from the classroom.

The teachers were aware of the vulnerability of the profession to outside influences and the repercussions of the BSE scare, foot and mouth epidemics and various international conflicts were always a threat to their security of employment.

The teaching was often very demanding. Our special courses, in particular, required a great deal of preparation and teaching of a high order and the teaching staff under the direction of Julian Lewis always responded to the challenges presented.

Our long serving and loyal year-round teaching staff.

From left: Martin Goddard, Ian Puffett, Daimon Adams , Chris Durrant, Director of Studies, Julian Lewis, Kathryn Gaye, Richard Farmer, Lynne Allenby, Jane Lewis.

Chapter 10   Social Activities

The importance of arranging out of school activities for our students was apparent long before we ran courses for teenagers. While the City did have a cinema and two theatres, the only other obvious places to go in the evenings were pubs. Our Scandinavian students in particular were attracted by the concept of pubs. The mere name seemed to imply a certain degree of "naughtiness" to those enduring state imposed regulation of public consumption of alcohol. However, since the majority of our adult students were female, there were few who dared venture into public houses alone or even in a group.

In recognition of this, we arranged at least one "pub evening" each week where Barbro and I made an appearance and spent an evening with the students. These occasions were always worthwhile and appreciated by the students, but they could be embarrassing for us too. Many a time we found ourselves outnumbering the locals in a pub as ten to fifteen of our students sat all evening with a glass of water or a coke, which we had bought for them. Landlords did not make a fortune from our business. That is not to say that occasionally a big drinker did not come along. The result of an evening in the pub for a very few could be the need for a taxi home, or as happened on one spectacular occasion, a ride home in a police car. The latter case occurred when a lawyer from a large Swedish company over imbibed. His landlord was a policeman and for some peculiar reason, this man convinced himself that since he could not remember the way home, instead of taking a taxi, the most efficient transport would be a police car as the driver would surely know where his host lived. To this effect, he hailed a passing police car.

In the early days, we frequently combined family weekend outings with trips for students. Barbro would pack the girls into our car and follow Big Blue, our ancient minibus, as I drove students out for walks in the New Forest or visits to events. Big Blue was to eventually come to grief when our multi talented teacher and sometime social organiser, Martin Goddard, demonstrated that he did not have a gift for judging heights when he tried to enter the covered section of the central car park at speed, thus rearranging the profile of the minibus irreparably.

Bill Jennings, Social Activities Manager

As time went by, our adult social programme became more and more ambitious and successful, especially under the management of Bill Jennings. However, it was the programme for teenagers and juniors which later gave SSE its unique selling point and a considerable amount of repeat business.

As described elsewhere in these memoirs, our first efforts at developing a social programme for young learners were fairly rudimentary. However, it was not long before we recognised that afternoon and also evening activities were an essential part of the course package. Each summer we appointed social organisers to run events. Year on year the number grew until in 2006 Bill Jennings was managing up to sixteen staff who were running the programme for homestay students and Anna had at least five running the residential programme.

The actual programme evolved using whatever facilities we could identify in the City. However, in the early days when we could squeeze all of our young students into the common room at Rollestone Street, there is no doubt that the most popular activity was the Song Evening. Nick McIver's magic with the guitar and in particular his rendition of "No Woman No Cry" were hugely appreciated. Even the Principal took a turn, usually with a boisterous audience participation number the most popular of which was "Swimming, Swimming in the Swimming Pool".

In those days the Social Organisers generally did a good a job of ensuring maximum enjoyment of events arranged on a shoe string budget. They themselves contributed greatly to the programme with plays and songs of topical interest. This included slightly irreverent ditties about the management and students.

I wish that I had kept the complete words of the 1984 school smash hit which started:

To be a social organiser,
You have to be a very early riser.
Shake the dreams from your head,
Get up from your bed,
Get up, get up,
Before Mike Wills is wiser.

I did keep this one however, sung to the tune of "Wild Rover":

I've been a wild student for three weeks or more.
And I've spent all my money on Wimpys galore.
Now Salisbury I'm leaving for a far distant shore
And I never will play the wild student no more.

Chorus
And its goodbye Salisbury
No nay never no more
Will I play the wild student
No never no more.

I went to a Wimpy I used to frequent
And told the waitress my money was spent,
I asked her for credit. She answered me nay.
Such custom as yours I can get any day.

Chorus

I then took from my pocket twenty pounds bright
And the waitress's eyes opened wide with delight.
She said I have burgers and chips of the best
And what I just told you was only in jest.
Chorus

I'll go home to my parents, they'll ask what I have done
I'll tell the coach trips and shopping were fun.
I spoke much more English than ever before
And I'll never forget it, of that I am sure.

Chorus

The adult students sometimes arranged events themselves. One of the most popular was when Cesare Cecchi, as part of his course, arranged a simulation of an activity which he often had to do professionally – a wine tasting.

Our Scandinavian students in particular enjoyed this occasion. Though in contrast to the others, they did not spit the sample wines into the buckets after tasting. At the end of the tasting Cesare carefully put the buckets behind an armchair so that they would not be spilt. There they were forgotten all weekend. On Monday morning when we arrived, the school smelt like a brewery.

I have always been keen on involving students in sports activities and in view of the fact that there was, at that time, very poor provision of sports facilities in the City, we decided to create our own. I managed to borrow some canoes, archery equipment and a climbing wall and badgered a reluctant District Council into letting us use a sports field by the River Avon. I appointed qualified instructors for the three activities and we added what we called "Adventure Activities" to our programme. It was not long however, before we ran into conflict with the most powerful lobby group in the area – the anglers. Our use of the river for canoeing was hugely resented by the fishermen who made representations to the Council. Eventually we had to stop this activity. Archery was abandoned for another reason, the proximity of pedestrians and dogs to the field we used, not to mention over enthusiastic students ignoring instructions, made the activity just too adventurous.

As numbers of students increased so did the range of activities, despite our unfortunate experience with "adventure activities". A feature of our programme was that we offered students a choice of up to six afternoon activities for homestay students and a similar number for residential students. This recognised the fact that children have different interests, but also that with the high number of students in the School, there had to be many activities to ensure that there were sufficient resources for all to take part.

Activities ranged from art classes where only a few students could participate to major sports tournaments where large numbers attended.

The philosophy which we developed and marketed, was that students should be kept active doing things which they enjoyed. We also wanted to know where our students were, that they were properly supervised and thus we could maximise student security.

This philosophy went down well with new and returning clients and our numbers grew every year.

The juniors' barbecue

In 2006 for most of July we had over six hundred and fifty young learners at the school, roughly half in residential accommodation. Adding to this the number of adults, around fifty, and the hundred and fifty or so students studying in Weymouth, the planning of activities was a significant logistical challenge.

We had realised early on that there was an inherent danger in allowing children to be unsupervised in the evenings. Thus we created an evening activity programme which was designed to cater for very large numbers. Most evenings all of the students attended the same activity, the ones who did not were the Junior students aged six to twelve. They had their own appropriate evening programme.

The evening activities for the majority of students repeated each week but this did not diminish their popularity.

Monday - Disco

Tuesday - Barbecue in the New Forest

Wednesday – Sports Evening

Thursday – Disco

Friday - Sports Evening

Bill and one of his teams

Pivotal to our evening programme was that we arranged transport for all the homestay students to get home after the event. Each evening a fleet of hired minibuses and our own three buses, ferried students direct to their host families. The distribution of students in buses destined for different parts of the town was a triumph of Bill Jennings' organisation and the fact that usually all three hundred and fifty homestay students were at their houses before 23.00 was remarkable. I acted as "sweeper" giving lifts to the few students whose accommodation was off the planned bus routes. There were of course a few students who would have liked to have made their own way home, dallying on the way. This was never allowed.

The big event of each summer was the Fancy Dress Party. This was a spectacular occasion and staff and children all participated to make it the main photo opportunity of the summer. Most staff and many children hired costumes from the costume hire shop at the theatre but a surprising number made their outfits or brought them with them from home. Returning group leaders briefed their children about the event and the Spanish groups in particular often had "group identity" team outfits.

Fina Coll, Estrella Osuna,
Tony Blair and Chus

The junior students at Godolphin usually made costumes as part of their craft activities and at the appointed time, paraded through the town to the City Hall, where the event took place, to join the older students for part of the evening.

This was the one and only time that all the students were assembled together. From the stage where I presented the prizes, the sight was awesome. Over six hundred students and staff, most of them in colourful costumes, were singing and dancing together. It was then, that the full realisation of what Barbro and I had created, from the simple beginnings, really hit me. The feeling of pride was of course tempered by the recognition of the enormous responsibility we had for all these young people.

The Wills family, Anna, Barbro, the Principal, Sarah and Emma

We were very fortunate that the majority of group leaders who brought children to the school were prepared to take part in all the activities and to encourage their students by example. This sometimes went beyond the call of duty. Several of our Italian groups were led by nuns. One of them, sister Redenta, was to be seen twice a week on horseback, in full habit, leading a student ride. Incidentally, this same leader tried to start a crusade in Salisbury to feed the poor. She collected in any uneaten food from her students' packed lunches and wandered around the City looking for needy souls who might be hungry.

Group leaders were hugely supportive of all events and in particular the Fancy Dress Party. It is not only children who enjoyed dressing up!

When the numbers of students at the School were relatively small, we usually arranged a farewell party for each group on their last evening. However, as numbers increased this became impossible to manage and we almost abandoned the tradition. Almost, that is, except for the Japanese groups. To them it was an essential part of their course and so on the final evenings for all these groups, be they adults or children, summer or winter, we arranged a special evening, often together with their host families. At these parties an important ingredient was generous helpings of chocolate cake washed down with Coca Cola. The best groups arranged almost everything themselves, dances, songs, quizzes and occasionally chopstick or origami lessons. However, quite a lot of input was necessary from school staff. This included sketches, games and inevitably, a rendition of "I'm Leaving on a Jet Plane". The effect the latter had was always the same, a room full of tearful Japanese and often, host families, for strong bonds had usually been forged. In fact, it was not until we retired that we realised the extent to which Salisbury host families had kept in touch with their past Japanese students and in some cases travelled to Japan to meet their families.

An important part of the social programme was the weekend excursions. As part of our policy of keeping children busy and directly under our control, we always included two weekend excursions, one on Saturday and one on Sunday. Further, we gave clients a menu where they choose their excursions, in advance, from a list of options. This was much appreciated by clients, but presented a major challenge to the Social Activities Manager. He had to arrange adequate transport and staffing for a range of different destinations each weekend day and make bookings for attractions. Inevitably, some clients changed their minds about their preferred excursion even as late as Friday, but it was our policy to give the clients what they wanted so there were often frantic reorganisations of bookings.

Through much of the School's history I saw the excursion coaches off on Saturdays and Sundays. This may seem to have been interfering in the duties of staff to whom responsibilities had been delegated, but in fact, it was frequently necessary to help marshal the large number of travellers and ensure that they got on the right buses. It was a relief when we appointed a transport manager to do this work.

It was quite a sight to see up to ten coaches and minibuses all departing the coach park for different destinations and despite the work and expense in making all the arrangements for this, it did mean that we knew where our students were and that they were properly supervised. That is not to say that there were not dangers involved and the need for our social organisers to be vigilant. It is a tribute to the organisers on the buses that there were very, very few mishaps. Those that there were, usually involved students getting lost, but not only students! On more than one occasion over-confident group leaders got lost in London.

The biggest worry was road accidents. In view of the number of excursions and transfers through the years, we were remarkably lucky in this respect. At one time we thought that there had been an accident. It was a terrifying experience. One Saturday afternoon we got a phone call from the police to say that a coach full of Italian students on the road from Bath had been involved in a collision with a lorry. There had been serious injuries and at least one fatality, the survivors were at the police station. We had had an excursion to Bath on that day and so we raced off to the police station to aid identification of the casualities and to help wherever we could. When we got there we found that the group was not ours, but that they had travelled from Southampton to Bath. One of the teachers had been killed and the other one was injured, so the group had no responsible adult to help them contacting parents and so on. The police had given over their leisure room to the uninjured students while they tried to trace the group organisers. The immediate need was for interpreters to establish details of the survivors and to take witness statements. Fortunately, we were able to mobilise a number of adult students and some of our own group leaders to help with this.

This was a most harrowing experience for all concerned, but my abiding memory of the tragedy was the effect when a policeman, keen to find a distraction for the students, put an Italian football match on the television in the lounge. The sounds of the children cheering their team while, not far away, in the old city hospital, some of their number were undergoing emergency operations, I found most discordant.

However, we were not immune from traffic dangers either. On one occasion on the motorway, a wheel from a caravan being towed in front of one of our coaches broke loose and hit the coach. Fortunately, the bouncing wheel missed the coach windscreen and embedded itself in the grill. The driver was able to stop without incident. The most serious accident happened one September while Barbro and I were on holiday. Anna was managing the School in our absence. She phoned to tell us that a coach, returning from London had had to swerve to avoid a car not far from Salisbury. The coach had ploughed through a hedge and ended up in a field. The passengers had been very fortunate to escape serious injury; Bill had just sat down after going round the coach talking to students, he was very lucky not to have been thrown through the windscreen.

But there was one serious casualty, a person who should not have been there at all! One of the Italian group leaders had asked her headmaster if she could take her nine-year old son with her on the journey to England. He had refused her permission. This had not deterred the teacher and she took the boy anyway. This poor lad suffered a broken leg in the crash and unfortunately for the teacher, the news of his injury quickly reached the headmaster when other students involved in the accident started phoning home to report on what had happened. As a footnote to this, the driver of the car which the coach swerved to avoid was sent to prison for drunken driving and causing the accident.

As I mentioned above, ensuring that all of our young students were busy at weekends gave us the relief of knowing that they were all purposefully and safely occupied. It also meant that none of our youngsters were in Salisbury on weekend days. Thus, when the Dean of the Cathedral phoned me one Saturday morning to report that one of our students had been seen urinating in the Cathedral Close, I was able, with confidence, to say that if one of our students was urinating in a cathedral close, it would not be Salisbury.

I have mentioned that Barbro and I took part in most social activities in the early years of the school. When we could, we inveigled Anna into joining us, which she willingly did. Often the three of us went to the New Forest barbecue to assist Louis. On one such occasion, Louis having left to trundle back to Salisbury in the minibus with all the equipment and we having seen the students safely away at the end of the event in the coaches, the three of us returned to the barbecue hearth in the gathering dusk, to tidy the site and pack the remaining stores into our Volvo estate car. I had driven the car over the grass up to the hearth to make loading easier.

The barbecue site we had been using was at a place called the Portuguese Fireplace. Apparently, during the First World War, the site had been an encampment for Portuguese troops. There were remnants of a wall which had been the soldiers bake house and from this the site got its name. It was a picturesque area about two and a half miles west of Lyndhurst, deep in the forest by the side of a minor road.

 I do not recall who did it, but just before we were due to leave, one of us slammed closed the estate car rear door. For some reason, the car locked itself. The keys were hanging in the ignition; our torch and Barbro's handbag were on the passenger seat. By this time it was dark and getting quite cold. Our jackets were in the car and these were the days before mobile phones, we were completely stranded.

I tugged and pulled and tried every way to get the car doors open, but to no avail. I went down to the minor road to flag down any passing car, to try to get help, while Barbro and Anna huddled around the dying embers of the barbecue for warmth. After an hour or so I gave up, clearly there was no traffic on this road once the tourists had gone home.

I tried again to open the car but with no success. Desperate times call for desperate measures. I found a large rock and swung it with all my might against the driver's window. The stone just bounced off! After two more tries I decided to have a go at the windscreen. Same result, clearly what is said about the solidity of Volvo cars is correct.

Most of us live in urban conurbations where there is always some light pollution at night; seldom do we experience the kind of darkness which enveloped us in the middle of the forest. It was so dark that only with difficulty could we now find our way back to the road. We abandoned the car and started walking together towards Lyndhurst. Several times we heard animals crossing the road in front of us, usually ponies but perhaps deer too. It was just after one o'clock that we found a phone box on the outskirts of Lyndhurst, but of course we had no money to make a phone call. I telephoned my father, reversed charge, and he agreed to call the Automobile Association, of which we were members, to come to the Portuguese Fireplace to break into our car.

Now of course we had to walk all the way back to the barbecue site to wait for the AA van to arrive. Soon after three in the morning, the AA man used a piece of bent wire and in several seconds had the car unlocked for us. What a comfort it was to put jackets on and have a snack of the spare barbecue bread rolls!

Another adventure was just as traumatic. For many years our social programme included rowing on the river. We hired rowing boats from a riverside pub adjacent to the coach park, called the Boat House. One year, in May, after all the summer course students had received their programmes which showed the activities to be provided, I received a phone call to say that the Boat House had gone into administration and was closed forthwith. This meant that we would not have access to the rowing boats. Since it would be very embarrassing to have to inform clients that the activity was no longer available, I decided to see if the situation could be rescued. I contacted the liquidators and explained my dilemma. They were helpful and said that they had no objection to us using the boats if we could agree a fee. However, they suggested that first I should check the craft to see that they were all sea worthy. They informed me that the boats had been lifted from the river and had been placed inside the pub. Further, they said that since the electricity had been cut off, I should take a torch.

I arranged with the liquidators to get a set of keys to the Boat House from the estate agents who were to handle the disposal of the building. Armed with these I unlocked the gates to the pub garden and then the door to the riverside entrance. A weird sight awaited me. There inside the pub in the gloomy room, were six rowing boats in stacks of two, but most disconcerting was the fact that the pub seemed to be in some kind of time warp. The drinkers' glasses were still on tables, many with drinks still in them, and the ash trays were full. It was as if all the people had been hastily turned out without being able to finish their drinks.

Suddenly, I heard a noise, the place was very eerie and though I was bit nervous, I convinced myself that what I had heard must be a rat. Then there was another noise, closer to me. I turned round and there in front of me was a man wielding a carving knife.

"'oo the 'ell are you?" he shouted.

I waved the bunch of keys and blurted that I had permission from the estate agent to enter the premises. He was unconvinced.

"What ya doin' 'ere?" he demanded.

I told him that I had come to look at the boats. He put the knife down and gave one of the boats a kick.

"They ain't no bloody good mate."

By this time I had lost all interest in the rowing boats and attempted to make my escape, which fortunately I was able to do. I sped back to the estate agents and told my story. Later I heard that the man I had been accosted by was the pub's chef. He had been illicitly squatting in the living quarters over the pub.

I decided that I would rather face the wrath of clients disappointed about the cancellation of rowing than to try to further negotiate the use of the boats.

Chapter 11   The long arm of the law

Our main worry about students was always their safety and security. In the earlier years of the School, Salisbury was anything but an international city. Indeed, if there was ever any problem with a foreigner, the police always contacted us, their assumption being that the person concerned was one of our students. Of course, this was not always the case, and we did get involved in helping the police with their enquiries about foreign visitors to Salisbury on several occasions by supplying interpreters.

Unfortunately, there being no real tradition of hosting foreigners in the City, there were a number of incidents where our students fell afoul of xenophobia, in particular among young people. In the first few years there were several occasions when our students were assaulted by locals. Fortunately, this phenomenon decreased through the years, as it became more common to see foreign visitors in the City.

The worst and most harrowing assault was that on an Italian boy who was beaten by a gang of English teenagers, one of whom was wielding a stick. Despite an emergency operation, our student lost the sight of one eye. This was a disaster for the boy, for his group leader and of course enormously upsetting for all the other students in the School. We were very keen to demonstrate to the boy's classmates and to others in the School that the police were taking this attack seriously and of course we wanted the assailants to be apprehended so that students could be assured that such an incident would not happen again. A major police investigation failed to identify the culprits and it began to look as if they were giving up when one day, two of the girls who had been with the boy when he was attacked, rushed into my office to tell me that they had seen one of the gang walk past the school.

What was I to do? What I did do could probably have landed me in prison! I ran out and apprehended the boy; I told him I was making a citizen's arrest. That did not make too much of an impression on him. I opened my wallet and flashed my Swedish driving licence at him intimating that it was a police warrant card. Why the Swedish driving licence? It had my photo on it and in those days it was very unusual to have a photo ID in England. I took the boy by the arm and led him back to the School and sat him in my office. While this had been going on my secretary had phoned the police.

It took an age for the police to arrive. Each time the boy got up enough courage to try to leave the office I threatened him more loudly. Eventually, I was able to hand him over to the police and through him they were able to identify and charge a gang member with grievous bodily harm. This was a most distressing episode, made more so when we discovered that the father of the victim of the attack had lost an eye when he was a boy.

However, as I have related elsewhere, there were occasions when it was our students who were the subjects of police action. One of the most bizarre but memorable of these involved a man in his thirties on one of our teacher refresher courses.

One afternoon, in the mid nineties, I was in the reception when a police car stopped outside the School. Two policemen got out of the car and walked towards the door with the teacher between them.

Clearly something was very wrong, so I quickly ushered the three of them into a vacant classroom on the ground floor. As Welfare Officer, Barbro joined us, as did the university lecturer who had brought the group of teachers to us.

We were to learn that the man had been arrested in a house in the Cathedral Close. The story unfolded that he had walked into the home of an elderly lady, gone upstairs and run a bath. She had gone up to investigate the noise and found a naked stranger in her bedroom, not surprisingly, she had called the police.

After some questioning, the man claimed that he had thought that the house was a brothel. He had gone in to use the services offered. Clearly, this explanation was greeted with some incredulity by the police. Barbro calmly tried to get the man to explain why he had thought the house was a brothel, his reaction was to make a move towards her and shout that he was going to kill her. A policeman restrained him, but the man turned to the officer and made the same threat to him. Out came the handcuffs and the interview ended.

It was not a welcome sight to see one of our course participants marched out of the School in handcuffs, but we were well pleased to be rid of him. We heard later that after two months in the local mental hospital he had been repatriated to his own country.

Our meetings with the police were by no means restricted to day time, on more occasions than I wish to remember, we met them at night. It was a condition of our insurance policy that we should have a monitored burglar alarm system. Each evening when we left the School we set the alarm and each morning whoever arrived first used their own personal code to deactivate the system. In the event that the alarm was triggered by an intruder a signal was sent to a security centre. Staff at this centre would then telephone our home number to warn that a break-in was taking place and they would also alert the police. Outside of the building was an acoustic alarm which would loudly announce that the alarm had been triggered. However, the acoustic alarm was cleverly programmed so that it was not set off until twenty minutes after a break-in had been detected. This gave the police time to reach the premises before the intruder had realised that the alarm had been raised.

It was most embarrassing not to say inconvenient that occasionally there were false alarms and they always seemed to happen right in the middle of the night. If we got a phone call in the small hours we knew immediately what had happened. We knew too that we had twenty minutes to get to the School before the acoustic alarm began to sound, waking the whole street. On most occasions we were able to avoid this happening.

When we arrived at the School a police car would be waiting outside for the key holder to arrive. We would unlock the outside door, turn off the alarm and then rush around the building with the police, looking for a possible intruder.

False alarms could be caused by a number of things, a window left open might cause a blind to flap, a picture on a wall might fall down during the night and so on. All of these call outs were embarrassing, but the police were generally very understanding. However, on one occasion as I turned the light on in a classroom I found a most unexpected visitor, a bat. Where it came from or how it got in I do not know, but clearly we had to get rid of it so that we could reset the alarm. A policeman warned me that bats were a protected species and we must be careful not to injure the creature, whereupon two officers spent half an hour before they managed to capture the intruder.

On a later occasion, Barbro and I arrived at the School at 03.00 and let the police in to search the building. Together we searched each room without finding anything untoward and then the police left. After they had gone, the two of us had another search and then spent a while in the office as we tried to contact the security centre to have the alarm reset. There seemed to be some tightening of controls because the person at the security centre refused to reset the alarms unless we could give a reason for the false alarm. This we could not, so we agreed to leave the system inactive until the morning when an engineer would come to check the system. We locked the building and returned home to our beds.

Next morning at 07.30 while on my way to work I received a phone call from Bob Dawson, our stalwart caretaker, to say that we had had a burglary, the office was in chaos and the till had been stolen. This was unpleasant enough, but then we realised that all the while Barbro and I had been in the building during the night, after the police had left, the burglar or burglars were hiding inside and not far away as they had obviously heard that we were not resetting the alarms!

Chapter 12   Milestones

As a profession, Teaching English as a Foreign Language is much under-respected and its contribution to the UK economy and to furthering international relations is barely recognised. From the beginning, we wanted to run a school with the highest standards we could aspire to, and for the market to recognise this. But we were also very keen that our enterprise should gain the respect of people in the City, the authorities and businesses. As regards gaining the respect of the general population, we had a strong lobby with our three hundred and fifty host families, all of whom could see that we treated them fairly and that our students were satisfied with their school experience.

Unfortunately, through the years, the influx of language students, staying in the UK temporarily, has been severely muddled with issues concerning immigration. The confusion has been used for political ends and is exacerbated by the so called "popular" press. At a conservative estimate, we had more than thirty thousand students studying with us during our time at the School. We know that one Chinese student absconded, we know of one Japanese girl who married an English boy, but we also know that the others went home at the end of their courses and our host families saw this. So the accusation that language school students boost immigration never blighted our reputation in the City.

Despite the parlous state of the School in the early years, it was not long before there was general recognition in the City that we were a legitimate business and that we made a positive commercial contribution to the area. By 1985 I found myself on a committee involved in tourism related interests in the City and a member of the Chamber of Commerce and Industry. A year later I was elected onto the Chamber Council. These activities took some time out of my working day and certainly many evenings, but I was glad to participate as I felt pride that our enterprise was recognised in this way.

The Chamber Council was a great learning experience for me. If I can refer back to my thirteen years abroad, I was well aware that I had been functioning all of that time either speaking Swedish or very "filtered" English, that is to say that in my teaching and in social situations I had to simplify my language to suit the listener's ability. After such a long period doing this and on returning to England, I became aware that my own English ability had suffered! My vocabulary had become limited; many words had passed from my active vocabulary into my passive vocabulary. Thus it was that when, initially, I was put in public speaking situations, for example presenting an argument in the Chamber Council, I had to overcome a near terror that I would not be able to express myself in a sufficiently sophisticated way to keep the respect of my colleagues. However, I quickly gained in confidence and clearly I must have made some impression as in 1990 I was elected

The whole family attended the Chamber President's dinner

President of the Chamber. This was a major feather in the cap of the School and recognised that we had forged a respected place in City life.

As a footnote to the above, this concern about my own English led me into a habit, which I still indulge in today, of collecting "difficult" and seldom used words. I make lists of them which I display next to my computer and when appropriate, try to use them.

Soon I became more involved in pressure groups whose purpose was to get proper District Council recognition of the importance of tourism in the south of the county and to get support for promotion and improvement of facilities. My main partner in driving these issues was Ian Newman, a larger than life undertaker. Together we started a campaign, Salisbury a City of Flowers, to enhance the City with floral decorations. Our scheme involved getting local businesses to contribute to an annual floral fund and using Ian's considerable persuasive power to cajole the District Council into paying an amount matching that donated by the business community, into the fund. The scheme became so successful that the Council eventually took over the running of it.

However, we were not satisfied that enough resources were being put into promoting the area and improving other facilities, so in 1994 Ian and I initiated a partnership with the Council called Tourism 2000. I was elected Chair, a position I held for five years. The partnership developed and became a blueprint for similar organisations in other parts of the county. The scheme still prospers today, though under another name.

Perhaps it was a tribute to my lack of partisanship as Chair that when I relinquished the job in 2000, I was approached first by the Conservative Party and then by the Labour Party to see if I would consider putting my name forward for election to the District Council!

And so we had achieved a certain respected standing in the City. However, the School was growing fast and it was necessary for me to focus totally on my professional duties. I left public life to immerse myself wholly in the interests of the business.

The School gradually gained some recognition in the profession. We were however in a very isolated position. Unlike towns where there was a concentration of language schools, we were, apart from the occasional appearance of short-lived competitors, geographically isolated. Having no colleague schools in the City and indeed no contacts whatever with any other schools, all of our teaching and administrative systems and our course programmes were self grown and unique to us. We were therefore rather nervous about presenting ourselves for inspection

Robert Key MP, a great supporter of the School, at our tenth anniversary party

for British Council recognition, (subsequently called accreditation). We had no yard stick by which to judge whether we might fulfil the criteria and reach the standards of the recognition scheme. Yet we were coming under increasing market pressure to be able to promote ourselves as British Council recognised.

In 1987 we applied to join the recognition scheme and on 19th August two inspectors duly appeared and conducted a two day inspection. Below are the last pages of the inspector's report. It should be pointed out that at every subsequent three yearly inspection Barbro's department always scored an "A" grade but on this occasion she was severely embarrassed when the inspectors, randomly choosing host families to visit, chose one lady who, fearing that the inspectors might think that she was too restrictive, announced that her teenage guests could stay out as late as they liked!

> The actual teaching seen was in line with the study programmes. Much of it was first class and none less than very satisfactory, with students fully participating in lessons. The use of aids and supplementary material was good. No one-to-one teaching was taking place at the time of the inspection but the quality of the other teaching seen clearly indicates that it will be of a similar or even higher standard.
>
> The School also offers courses on methodology, materials production and language improvement for teachers of English and while no such course was in progress at the time of the inspection the Inspectors were favourably impressed by the evidence of the work done on such courses. Although it is (possibly) outside the brief of the present inspection, we were interested to hear that the School is thinking about starting RSA TEFL courses. We consider that it is well equipped in both human and material resources to undertake such courses which would not only offer training facilities to the School's own staff – where these were needed, but would undoubtedly have a general beneficial spin-off to the School – as do its present teacher training courses.

RECOMMENDATION

We strongly recommend recognition in categories (i) and (ii).

GRADES

MANAGEMENT	A
PREMISES AND RSOURCES	A
STAFF	B+
WELFARE	B-
TEACHING	B+

Having gained recognition, in 1991, and after being invited to do so several times, we applied for membership of the Association of Recognised Language Schools, (ARELS). The reason for our delay in applying was partly due to financial reasons, but also because one of the requirements was that a candidate school should be able to furnish a recommendation from another member school. Since we did not know any other schools, this requirement was eventually circumvented by the Chairman of ARELS, Brian Heap, paying us an inspection visit.

As a member of ARELS, the School was invited to join the local association of language schools in the south of England, the Recognised Language Schools Association in Wessex. This really brought us out of geographical isolation as I now had the chance to meet representatives of many schools, mainly from Bournemouth and Poole. I was quickly to learn however, that relationships between the member schools were not the most harmonious. It was perhaps because I was an unpartisan outsider, that two years later I was elected to chair this organisation.

Thus it was that by 1991, we were firmly established as a respected member of the Salisbury business community and we had achieved recognition within our profession. My involvement with ARELS developed as I was elected to the Council of the organisation in 1998 and, eventually, I was proud that as representative of the Salisbury School of English I became first Chair of ARELS and then Co-Chair of the greatly enlarged national association, English UK, in 2004. It was a huge honour to follow in the footsteps of such EFL notables as Timothy Blake, Charles Harrison and Richard Day. It was also a privilege to work with the Chief Executive, Tony Millns.

It is true to say that our school with such humble beginnings, was eventually represented at the very pinnacle of the profession.

The school administration staff in the late nineties.

From left to right: Louise Crook, Bill Jennings, Anna Wills, Barbro Wills, Sandy MacIntyre and Kerstin Rood

Chapter 13   The Final Years

Each year, apart from years when there was some international concern such as the BSE scare or foot and mouth contagion, the School grew. And each year we increased our facilities. We had recognised early on that we needed an alternative destination to offer to students we could not accommodate. We also saw it as important to be able to offer another product to existing clients who might like to have a change from Salisbury. In this way we hoped to keep their business. As early as 1990 we had opened a summer centre in Exmouth, a year later we had a course in Exeter.

There were, however, difficulties in finding classrooms in these places and also in administering the courses at distance with our very limited resources. Noting the demand for residential accommodation, as mentioned elsewhere, we started courses in a private school in Bruton, this was in 1995. However, I had long had a dream of running courses on the Isle of Wight, so when the opportunity to rent

Upper Chine School,
Shanklin, Isle of Wight

Upper Chine School in Shanklin arose, I was delighted to let Anna open a summer residential centre there.

It was a delightful place and perfect as a contrasting alternative to Salisbury. We ran courses there in the summers of 1996 and 1997 and at Easter 1997.

It looked as if we had established a permanent alternative summer venue to Salisbury, but in July 1997 I was summoned to Ryde School, the owners of Upper Chine, to be told that the whole estate was to be put up for sale. It was a considerable property with a number of substantial Victorian houses and extensive grounds as well as the main building. I did not have the wherewithal to make an offer, so I tried to interest our main Japanese agent, a wealthy educational trust, in a joint venture. Unfortunately, they had recently bought another private school in East Anglia and were not interested.

THE ISLE OF WIGHT ENGLISH COLLEGE

RESIDENTIAL ENGLISH COURSES

The Isle of Wight English College is a branch of IS England Ltd. owners of the Salisbury School of English

That I did not find a way to purchase this estate is to my eternal regret, especially as I learnt later that the eventual buyer had bought the property in instalments, thus giving him the opportunity to develop parts to finance the next instalment and so on.

Our need for an alternative summer centre still existed and so, in 2001, we started homestay courses in Weymouth. Eventually, we split this activity off from SSE and registered it as a separate company, Weymouth English Centre, with its own British Council accreditation. Thus, as my 62nd birthday approached in the summer of 2004 our business enterprise was in good health. Our residential and homestay courses in Salisbury were full and we had a growing summer business in Weymouth. The company was well in profit though, as normal, we never took a dividend out of the business, but reinvested every last pound in promotion and improving and expanding our facilities.

But I was acutely aware that I and indeed Barbro too, had been incredibly lucky in that we were both very healthy and fit; the question was how long we could expect to be so. Our work was increasingly demanding as the business grew and through the last ten years or so it became all consuming. Fortunately, we had a very stable family, our girls were tremendously supportive, all of them working for greater or lesser lengths of time, for the business. Anna had focused her life on the language school business while Emma and Sarah helped out when they could.

It was a huge benefit to us that the girls were so close to us in every way, as we did not have any other social life to speak of. In fact, apart from the several agents who had become friends and some friends still from our time in Sweden, we had only two or three close friends in England, despite having lived here for a quarter of a century. We were just so unavailable to people who tried to befriend us. Our business lives were so busy that we could seldom accept invitations, or if we did, our visits were likely to be interrupted by phone calls or by us rushing off for appointments.

With the benefit of hindsight I see clearly now that our business model suited a small enterprise, but for a burgeoning summer enterprise it was flawed. We had built our business on an extremely high level of personal involvement. We, that is Barbro, me and from June 1996, Anna and later her husband Mike, were always available to clients and staff, we took part in most activities from parties to meeting and greeting groups. For example, one, two, three or all of us met every single group arriving at Salisbury coach station to personally welcome them and put leaders at ease. Similarly, we did the same thing on departure, we were always there to say goodbye no matter how uncivilised the hour, and ensure that students got away safely. In summer 2006 there were around 40 group

arrivals and the same number of departures from Salisbury coach station and another 20 or so at Godolphin or St Mary's. This was a huge undertaking, yet it was a vitally important component in building good relations with new clients and returning group leaders had an expectation of such attention.

In fact planning the whole business of transferring students became a significant part of my summer work. Group transfer planning was the easy part; we usually knew the flight details well in advance. The most complex part was arranging transfers for the large number of individual students, some of whom were as young as eight. Frequently, parents were slow in giving us flight details.

Courier Emma supervising "meeting and greeting"

Once having got all the flight details of arrivals I planned the work of our team of couriers. Their work was very important. I have previously mentioned, my mantra was "You only get one chance to make a first impression". The couriers were all uniformed and well supervised by our superb transport manager, Kelvin Chambers. The couriers included his wife, Angela, and also Emma Wills, who regularly gave up part of her summer holiday and weekends to help. The same team ensured that students caught their departure flights.

As regards accommodation, the increasing number of homestay students put an ever growing burden on Barbro. Her philosophy was that there is always a bed; it is just a matter of finding it. She never compromised and maintained the same high standards no matter how difficult it was to find accommodation. But this took its toll. Each year, from the beginning of May onwards we worked in the office in the evenings as well as in the day times. Around eight o'clock I would go out to buy food for an evening meal and the three of us, and occasionally other late working staff, would dine in the common room. Afterwards I would go off to visit the evening activities and to help out with the ferrying home of children, leaving Barbro and often Anna, to work late. And it was usually very late, with Barbro returning home in the small hours. This routine continued through until the end of July, when, as our student numbers began to drop, we reached a magical day when host families began to ring Barbro to ask if there were any students needing accommodation!

Even with the unstinting help of our transport manager Kelvin, when we were at home, at weekends, there was a constant stream of calls from host families, worried parents and group leaders. It reached absurd proportions; we had to take it in turn to eat at mealtimes so that one person was always available without a mouthful of food, to answer the telephone!

It could be argued that we had not been successful in delegation of duties and there is merit in this view. However, apart from a precious few, very few, it was impossible to find capable staff who were prepared to work the inconvenient hours required of our job. Besides, as I have already mentioned, the ethos of the company was that at least one of the owners would always be available to give personal service.

By 2004 it was clear to me that we must plan an exit strategy to leave the business while we were still fit enough to do so. For my part I had reached the apogee of my career, indeed from my diary I can identify the day when I felt that this point had been reached. On the 25th November 2004 as Co-Chair of English UK I attended the autumn conference. This was the first time that that there had a been a conference gathering of all the representatives of the private and public sector members, together with the movers and shakers of the TEFL profession. At the formal dinner for several hundred members I was persuaded to reintroduce the main entertainment of the old ARELS conference dinners by agreeing on the running of a sweepstake where members bet a pound each on how long the speaker would hold forth. The problem was that we had no speaker! With fifteen minutes notice I agreed to speak. Fortunately, my memory did not let me down and after a few serious words I was able to recall a sufficient number of jokes to receive the general approbation of the delegates when I resumed my seat. The lucky winner of the sweepstake had bet on twelve minutes and thirty five seconds.

To a large extent, Barbro had also reached the peak of her career, although accommodating all of our students in the summer of 2006 had to be her greatest achievement. However, there was another exciting prospect on the horizon which encouraged us to seek to have more time at our disposal and that was that by the time we had made our decision on the path to take, there was the prospect of becoming grandparents to Anna and Mike's first child.

In considering the best way to give up the responsibility for the running of the School, the obvious solution was to hand the business over to Anna to run, and for the three of us to retain ownership. However, we knew that this would be an unreasonable burden for her alone, especially as she was starting a family, and the temptation for us to help out would undoubtedly have prevented us from making a clean break.

Another solution which might make it possible for Anna to manage the business alone, or indeed for Barbro and me remaining in employment leading a less demanding life, would be to redefine our market. This plan was an attractive one. We would operate year-round for "commissioned" young learners' courses and teachers' courses, a growing part of our business, and grow our winter school for South Americans as well as our major summer season. We would abandon our loss-making year-round adult group courses, thereby easing the considerable administrative and economic burden they imposed. We had been offered the lease of a nearby church school, shortly to be totally refurbished, which had big classrooms suited to the planned activity. This building, St Martin's, would become the Salisbury School of English. Our intention then was to develop Fowlers Road as flats. I had already investigated this possibility in some detail and had been granted outline planning permission.

Anna and Mike Thatcher

Yet another possibility was to sell the business as a going concern. I had no idea what the School was worth or how to sell it. However, this course of action would not have guaranteed Anna continued employment, or if it did, she might well have difficulty in adapting to the business culture of a new employer. A solution to the latter problem presented itself from a much unexpected quarter.

In 1996, Anna had been employed in Sweden as an assistant to the Head of the English Department at the Folkuniversity in Stockholm. Applying both the skills she had learnt with us and our work ethic, she had made a very positive impression on her employers. Thus it was when, in 2005, the Principal of this Swedish organisation's English school for adults in Loxdale, near Brighton, announced his retirement that, unknown to me then, Anna was considered as a possible replacement.

The Swedish Chairman of the Board of the Loxdale School approached me and asked if I would be prepared to help to recruit the new Principal. I met him for lunch on 24th May to discuss the post and for me to get some background to the School. I was asked to advertise and then draw up a short list of candidates for interview. Very diplomatically he asked if Anna might be interested in the job, aware of course that she was in our employ.

After some discussion with Barbro and Anna we agreed that if Anna was offered this post and decided to take it, the field would be clear for us to sell the business. However, first I wanted to be certain that the proposed post would be a good prospect for Anna and so I carried out a detailed assessment of the organisation. If Anna were to be appointed to the post, it would mean a great upheaval for her family. Her husband Mike, who had also been employed by SSE for several years and son Oliver, would have to leave their comfortable cottage in Salisbury and move to Sussex. Not a decision to be taken lightly. The upshot was that Anna was interviewed for the post on 21st October 2005 and appointed. She took up the post in early 2006 with the condition that she would be able to work for us as centre manager at Godolphin through the summer of 2006.

In August 2005 the School was put on the market through an agent. We had decided to keep the Weymouth English Centre in our ownership. There were several reasons for this, perhaps the most bizarre one was that I really feared about how we would manage in retirement with so much spare time and I saw Weymouth as a sideline to keep us occupied.

Our first attempt to sell the School through an agency was unsuccessful and harrowingly so. This was not because there was lack of interest in the business, quite the contrary, we had many interested parties. One of the organisations wishing to buy the School had a branch in Salisbury. We informed the agent that we were not prepared to sell to them on any terms. A list of other potential purchasers was whittled down to two and these were invited to make an offer.

One of the two potential buyers made an offer slightly higher than the other and we agreed to proceed with the sale. The buyer was an organisation on the south coast, an institution for which we had much respect and one which we believed would run SSE in a manner that we would approve of. I should

Photo taken in summer 2006. The sign on the top right hand corner of the notice board reads – "Perfect planning prevents pathetic performance"!

mention that we had a major concern that all of our faithful and in many cases very longstanding clients should find the change of ownership seamless and that they could expect the new owner to aspire to the standards which we embraced. Similarly, we were keen that our long serving and loyal staff, Julian Lewis, Director of Studies and his teaching team should have their security guaranteed.

The lengthy legal process began and we supplied copious information to the buyer about our clients, our prices and so on. There was of course a confidentiality agreement between buyer and seller. On 24th October I received an e-mail from one of the owners of the organisation buying SSE. He had copied it to me by mistake. The e-mail was addressed to their solicitors stating that they were buying SSE together with the owner of the organisation which we had told the agent that we were not prepared to sell to. Clearly, we had been deceived! We cancelled the sale. The School was offered to IH WELS, the previously losing bidder, on the same terms and they enthusiastically accepted. The whole legal process had to start again. At this stage I involved our accountants, it was a mistake not to have done so before because they pointed out that we would need to transfer a large amount of money from SSE Ltd to the parent company, Wills International Language Services, as part of the settlement of inter-company accounts. We could not do this until summer 2006. So, in January I was forced to tell a disappointed IH management that we would have to postpone the deal until September. This meant too that B and I would have to manage the School through the next summer, our biggest ever with over 1400 students booked in Salisbury and Weymouth. That summer we had 135 employees on payroll.

As a positive side issue, it would mean that I could see out my full term as Co-Chair of English UK, which was due to end in May 2006.

The sale to IH WELS included an agreement that we would grant a lease on the use of Fowlers Road, an arrangement which we were very happy about. Negotiations with the prospective owners were cordial, as we got on well personally, and were concluded in good time for a change of ownership after the summer.

At 14.30 on Friday 1st September 2006 I received a phone call from my solicitor to say that the contracts were ready for signing to complete the sale. By 15.00 we had signed and the School was no longer ours. We returned to our offices and I cleared my desk.

At 18.30 I called in to see Barbro to say that I was ready to leave, however, the typically sedulous lady was not for leaving until she was absolutely certain that every last detail had been dealt with, I drove home and later Barbro walked.

It was all over, twenty-seven years work; we had had the satisfaction of creating a major player in the TEFL profession from the simplest of beginnings. Yes, it had been hard at times but the positives rendered the negatives negligible. We had had the privilege of working with some hugely talented and dedicated staff, the opportunity to visit many parts of the world, the honour of gaining the respect of many clients, but most of all we had touched the lives of tens of thousands of students, young and old and we hope, contributed positively to international understanding. When I think back to the days in early 1979 when the Salisbury School of English was but a figment of our imaginations, a dream, yet one which if it were to succeed, would require total dedication, I am hugely grateful that I was lucky enough to have a companion who, for better or worse, was prepared to embark on this great adventure and with equal determination, to see it through with me.

Until one is committed, there is hesitancy, the chance to draw back. Concerning all acts of initiative (and creation), there is one element of truth, the ignorance of which kills countless ideas and splendid plans – that moment one commits oneself, then providence moves all.
All sorts of things occur to help one that would never otherwise have occurred. A whole stream of events issues from the decision, raising in one's favour all manner of unseen incidents and meetings and material assistance which no man would have dreamed could have come his way. Whatever you can do or dream you can, begin it. Boldness has genius, power and magic in it. Begin it now

Goethe